GIPSY SMITH

Yours heartily
Gipsy Smith

GIPSY SMITH IN EARLY MIDDLE AGE. The evangelist
as thousands knew him

GIPSY SMITH
from the forest I came

David Lazell

MOODY PRESS • CHICAGO

Based on the British edition entitled

FROM THE FOREST I CAME

The Story of Gipsy Rodney Smith M.B.E.

© 1970 by David Lazell,

published by Concordia Publishing House Ltd., London

North American Edition

© 1973 by

THE MOODY BIBLE INSTITUTE

OF CHICAGO

ISBN: 0-8024-2959-9

Contents

CHAPTER	PAGE
Forward to American Edition	7
Forward to the British Edition	9
Preface to the American Edition	13
Author's Note	17
1. A Life Full of Surprises	19
2. Journey from the Forest	25
3. Cornelius, a Tale Told in Silver	33
4. Decision at Bedford	42
5. A Field Full of Turnips	50
6. Stone Walls	57
7. Revival at the Ice House	62
8. Dismissal	71
9. The Hero of Hanley	76
10. Faith That Goes Forth	84
11. The Converting Furnace	92
12. The Fruit at the Top of the Tree	101
13. The Children	108
14. The Bull's-Eye	115
15. The Preacher	124

16. Tomfoolery in Glasgow   129

17. The Miracle of Morchard Bishop   133

18. Bumps and Buffetings   140

19. Finding a Wife for Cornelius   146

20. We Have Seen Strange Things Today   153

21. Into the Twentieth Century   161

22. Harvest at Cape Town   168

23. Vote for Gipsy Smith—and No Beer   174

24. Ten Minutes Ahead of the Devil   178

25. A Handful of Memories   183

26. Ici On Parle Anglais   192

27. The Golden Years of Gipsy Smith   200

28. Full Circle   212

29. More Memories   218

30. Bells Across Elizabeth   228

31. A Very Special Romany   233

32. The Beloved Biographer   238

33. Mary Alice   245

    Epilogue   251

    Evaluation: His Ministry and Ours   253

Foreword to the American Edition

It is not easy to write a biography of a great Christian. Most biographies are either so complimentary that they read like press releases, or so critical and detailed that they tarnish the halo and bore the reader.

This biography of Gipsy Smith does not go to either extreme and for this reason ought to be read by every Christian who wants to get to know this colorful evangelist better. David Lazell presents the Gipsy as he was—a happy soul-winner who made the Christian life attractive to the man on the street. Not everybody appreciated his bubbling humor and his folksy ways, but God used him because he was totally committed to the winning of the lost to Jesus Christ.

Any book that encourages evangelism is worth reading, because a sincere burden for souls is greatly needed in many churches today. I believe that a careful reading of this book will help to make a man a better witness. I know what it did for my own heart, and for this reason I plan to reread it often.

An Englishman by birth, Gipsy Smith made at least thirty trips to the United States and was received with enthusiasm. It was on his last trip in 1947 that he was called home. It is time that Christians in the States become better acquainted with this unique servant of God, and I can think of no better way than the reading of this concise but interesting book.

As you read, expect something to happen to you.

WARREN W. WIERSBE

Moody Memorial Church
Chicago, Illinois

Foreword to the British Edition

David Lazell has told the story of my grandfather so well that it has personally given me great pleasure, and I feel proud that Gipsy Rodney Smith, Member of the British Empire, was my grandfather.

What did it mean to my brother Rodney and me, the English grandchildren, to have him as our grandfather? Did we find the man and the religion he preached true? I think we did.

As a child I had the joy of staying for weeks at a time in my grandparents' home in Cambridge. There in that atmosphere of peace and perfect order (for Granny was a wonderful housekeeper), I caught the feeling of preparation and waiting for Grandpa's return. Once Grandpa came home unexpectedly for Christmas from America, and I shall always remember the light in Granny's face as she said, "Your grandfather will be home in . . . days." What a busy and happy Christmas that was with all the family gathered together!

Grandpa's personality was such that when he was home, life somehow became more vivid, and all the family and household felt this. He was able by his presence to make every occasion into a special one, either grave or gay, and his joy in simple things, a family picnic, or showing me the nests of baby birds as a child, I shall never forget. We who saw him under all conditions both at home and in front of his vast audiences, truly admired and respected him, as well as loved him.

Both my brother and I made our public decision to follow Christ at Grandpa's meetings as children. Then as we reached our teens, we both to a greater or lesser degree experienced doubts, skepticism, and a youthful dislike of the atmosphere of evangelism. We were living in a changing world, we found there were people who did not go to church regularly; we were "goody goodies" with church twice on Sundays, plus Sunday school, and our family's nonparticipation in worldly things. My brother, I am sure—though he never talked about it—probably suffered quite a bit of teasing at his public school for being the Gipsy's grandson. However, increasing maturity and experience of life plus the prayers and personal witness of our parents restored our spiritual balance until, as the days went by, we could truly say, "This Jesus, we too also follow." My brother was a quiet, reserved, gentle man, of great integrity and sincerity, both in his work at the university and in his home and church life. His early death at forty-five deprived the world of one of God's quiet workers, and his wife and daughter of a loving husband and father.

At the close of Grandpa's American campaign in March, 1934, after addressing the Virginia Asher Business Women's Council, in Birmingham, New York, he was presented with a pocket New Testament. It was a beautiful little book, attractively bound in blue leather, gilt edged, and with colored Biblical pictures inside. When Grandpa came home that spring, it was put with lots of other papers on the table in the study where my childish eye fell upon it, and I asked if I

could have it. I was told, "Yes, but take care of it."
That little Testament lives in my overnight case and
goes with me on all my travels. The thing I treasure
most about it though, is the inscription on the flyleaf
which reads:

> To express our deep appreciation to Gipsy Smith
> Because: —
> You've lived the Beauty of Jesus here,
> You've made Himself and His Word more dear,
> You've filled our souls with a purpose true,
> The Beauty of Jesus in us to renew.

My dearest wish is that that might also be said of me.

Zillah Elizabeth Lean

Cambridge, England

Preface to the American Edition

This book got started one day in the spring of 1969. I was in Bath, the handsome Georgian city of England, when I almost stumbled over an old tub filled with equally old books outside an antique shop. Although I was on my way to a business appointment, I could not resist the temptation to examine the books. In any case, as my wife, Anne, and I enjoy reading on tape for the blind, I am always on the lookout for something unusual that may interest our blind friends. So I decided to buy an old green-covered book, published in 1902, about the life and work of Gipsy Smith. The book was just ten cents (one of the cheapest books I have ever purchased); and after it was thrust into my overcrowded briefcase, I resumed my way to the business conference.

I could not have imagined how that old book was to influence my life. The name of Gipsy Smith was almost unknown to me before I read the book, which I completed only a few days later. It seemed nothing less than astonishing that this simplehearted, imaginative, godly man was now seemingly forgotten. The old book told only the first forty years of the Gipsy's life. What happened after 1902 (when the book was published), I wondered. Did the Gipsy's great mission end abruptly, or did he fade into obscurity? Did anyone now remember him?

As I was unable to trace any books in print about the Gipsy, I wrote to one or two of the Christian papers here in England. Indeed, my letter inviting memories of Gipsy Smith was the very last letter to be printed in the late, lamented *Christian* newspaper, with one or two other published letters. It produced an avalanche of mail. With every mail delivery, I received stories of the Gipsy's ministry and expressions of thankfulness for his witness. Even then, however, the idea of writing a book did not occur to me. Instead, I suggested to a Christian publisher that he simply reprint the original life story which I had found at Bath with additional details to finish the story. However, he thought that no one would be interested.

By this time, the early summer of 1969, I was attempting to pursue a busy career in advertising and to handle an ever-increasing flow of mail. Every letter contained a story of some kind and required an individual reply. I was astonished to discover that Gipsy Smith, who had seemed such a Victorian figure, lived right up to 1947. Further, that there had hardly been an aspect of mass media (except television, then in its infancy) in which he had not been actively involved. As I write, I have at hand full-page articles in secular newspapers, in which Gipsy had rewritten some of his best-loved sermons. He possessed the common touch, the power to inspire through simple words and the sincere expression of the gospel.

I began to see that the Gipsy possessed that secret of successful communication which we so often debate and so often lack. Basically, he loved his congregations and was unafraid to show it. It was strange how, for me, the busy mass media world of our time related to the Gipsy's ministry. As I started to write

the inevitable book resulting from my research and **the** encouragement of those who knew him personally, I saw that people in our time are hungry for the personal approach, the personal touch.

Looking back, some two years or so after the publication of the British edition, I can see how my involvement with the Gipsy's mission was inevitable from the moment I stumbled over that old tub. The good Lord has a great sense of humor, it seems to me; and I could relate a number of events in which I was literally guided to material. It was as if the Lord was at my side, saying, "How about that, David?" Still, as Gipsy himself said, our ministry should be filled with glorious surprises.

I still am receiving mail from people who have read the book. Basically, they say much the same thing: our great lack today is not great excitement but great preaching—when we define great preaching as great themes simply and certainly expressed. The good example of Gipsy Smith and those of his contemporaries will come into their own in our generation, not because they have anything new to teach us but simply because, in a complex age, the gospel shines in its simplicity. And in that, the Gipsy would say, an education among the animals and trees of the forest may be as effective a training as one may find on the world's best campuses. He never despised learning and, like this writer, always loved books. It is a matter of recognizing the source of true power, and I hope you discover it afresh in this book which comes from the forest.

DAVID LAZELL

Bristol, England

A Gypsy Camp. A painting of the lane in which his mother died

Author's Note

The quotations at the beginning of each chapter are taken from the diary kept by Zillah, the Gipsy's daughter, during the South African tour of 1904. The caravan emblem is that of the design by Rodney Lean for the presentation made to the evangelist in 1936.

Letters quoted represent only a small part of the mail received by the author in his research, and he wishes to express his warmest thanks to all those who shared their memories of the campaigns. It would be impossible to name them all, but the author recognizes that this is their book as much as his, as far as real inspiration is concerned.

The Gipsy's two sons remained preachers to the end of their days. Hanley, after many years of devoted service as a Methodist minister, died in retirement at Moseley, Birmingham, in 1949. Two years later, Albany, resident in America, died at the age of seventy. He was known as "Gipsy Smith Jr.", having become an evangelist after working on trans-Atlantic liners and, later, a business career. One of Albany's most famous missions was at Poindexter Park, Jackson, Mississippi, in 1922. He was held in warm esteem throughout North America like his famous father.

Mrs. Zillah Lean was a loyal and cheerful Christian throughout her life. Gipsy Smith could well be proud of his three children. From the forest he came to go forth into the world and to give the world another generation of evangelists.

Miss Zillah E. Lean, the Gipsy's granddaughter, is a music teacher and singer, and lives at Cambridge, England, home of so many of the great events in this book.

All of us who have had a hand in the preparation of this book trust that you share our gratitude at being reminded of such great blessings given by God through the ministry of one man, Gipsy Rodney Smith, Member of the British Empire, and evangelist to the world.

1

A Life Full of Surprises

A dead fish can go with the stream, but it takes a living one to swim against it.

This book is full of surprises. As a matter of fact, as I begin writing it, I hardly know what will happen. Gipsy Smith was always a nonconformist, a man who loved surprises—and giving them! He would often begin one of his sermons like this: "I used to be in the timber business—I sold clothespins!" This was a reference to the days when, as a gypsy lad, he sold his wares, door to door. This statement brought more than laughter the time when an old lady called out, "And good clothespins they were, Gipsy. I've still got those you sold me."

Gipsy had an eye for what we call audience-involvement. He was always delighted to meet people who had known him as a boy.

"I started off by preaching to turnips," he said. "I was only sixteen, but they were a very attentive congregation."

We can only wonder what he said at those distant open air meetings among the vegetables. Not that Gipsy Smith had to worry about lack of attention

19

by his audiences. He could talk for well over an hour without any notes and still hold his congregation.

Once during an American campaign, he noticed a man wearing a heavy overcoat, sitting in the front of a very crowded hall. It was warm inside the building, and the Gipsy wondered why the man continued to wear the overcoat. However, the Gipsy talked for about an hour and a half before pausing to inquire of his audience, "Have you had enough?"

They did not reply, but the heavily clad man slowly rose and took off his overcoat, before sitting down with the words, "Now, let's have some more!"

To the end of his life, Gipsy Smith remained a simple, straightforward man who spoke from the heart. He remained humble, even if some of his critics suggested that, in later years, he tended to be theatrical. It may be that they expected the Gipsy to be solemn, but solemnity in the sense of a long face and measured tones was quite foreign to this man, born in a tent and raised among the hedgerows of nineteenth-century England.

When he paid a visit to Johannesburg, he received the ceremonial afforded a representative of the old country. "I let Mrs. Smith get into the carriage (the one which carried Lord Roberts during the South African War) and then I followed. I turned to the vast crowd and shouted, 'Here goes Lord Clothespins!'"

Sometimes, he showed the old knife which his father had used, long years before, to make the clothespins that he sold.

"Whenever the devil comes around to tell me what a great fellow I am, I show him this old knife, and tell him that I'd probably still be using it to make clothespins but for Jesus."

He never forgot his gypsy origins. Indeed, he liked nothing more than to visit a gypsy encampment. His hosts, at various campaigns, would tell him that gypsies were to be found just outside the town, and, at the first opportunity, Gipsy would set out to find them. Often, they proved not to be real gypsies at all, but the kind of "rough people who gave real gypsies a bad name" (as Gipsy himself put it). Yet, he was once found in a gypsy tent, singing to a true Romany baby, a look of utter delight upon his face.

Gypsies love children, and retain a childlike nature all of their lives. This must explain at least part of the story of Gipsy Smith, as it unfolds. He never became sophisticated; he always said what he meant in plain unmistakable terms; and he loved his congregations, even when he rebuked them. Maybe that love is not always so evident in these days of conventional sermons. What minister today would go into the pulpit, kneel, and weep for the sins of the people?

Who now would speak as he did, for example, at Southport, when he addressed a large gathering of high school girls and guides thus: "Oh, you beautiful young women, all in the prime of life, what can I do for you? I would lay myself prostrate on the floor of this church all through the night to see you converted."

The keynote of his sermons was the love of God, and it proved irresistible. At the Southport meeting, the girls lined up to reach the communion rail. As we shall see, the converts usually remained true to their decision. Gipsy Smith always attributed the work of the Holy Spirit to the right quarter. A Methodist

class leader approached the Gipsy at the close of a
successful campaign and somewhat sadly remarked
that he had, for years, prayed for the conversion of
various members of his class, but they had only come
to decision at the Gipsy's word.

The Gipsy, in his characteristic way, clasped the
class leader and reminded him that one sows, another
reaps but *God* gives the increase. Furthermore, the
Gipsy added, these people needed his care more than
ever now. Effective follow-up, the Gipsy always said,
was the real key to a campaign's success.

After the meetings, the Gipsy would "warm up the
bones" by sitting by a fire or standing with his back
to it. This, he explained, helped to keep away the
aches and pains. On one occasion, following a meeting, he was kneeling by the side of a fire in the vestry
"warming up the bones" when a steward entered.
Momentarily startled, the steward immediately knelt
by the Gipsy's side, convinced that the evangelist was
engaged in prayer.

He was, of course, a great man of prayer. Sometimes,
he startled his congregation by proceeding thus:

"If I came back for a campaign, would you bring
your unsaved friends?"

"Yes!" they replied.

"And would you support the campaign financially?"

"Yes!"

"And would you all come along to the midweek
prayer meeting?"

"Yes!"

"Then," declared the Gipsy, "if you would do all
that for me, why don't you do it for your own pastor?"

At one service, while talking about the lack of prayer

meetings, he turned to the host minister, and asked when the church was having its next prayer meeting. Thinking quickly, the minister responded, "We are going to announce a special one for tomorrow night!"

Gipsy Smith's ministry was as much for the church as for those outside it.

"People who don't read their Bibles read *you*," he said. "You are the Bible for many people—and I imagine that some of them look for a revised version."

How he yearned for revival! Nothing saddened him more than a church too respectable for revival.

"You might have a fine reputation down here," he sighed. "But one day you'll have to explain your stewardship to Him—and He's interested in revivals, not reputations."

It would be a masterpiece of understatement to call his campaigns memorable. Gipsy Smith went through the churches like a mighty roaring wind. He swept aside a lot of encrusted traditions and revolutionized the ministry of preaching.

"What we need in our ministry is an element of glorious surprise!" he said. "We should always expect something to happen when we preach the gospel."

Not everyone thought that way. As Gipsy related, his friend, Reverend Samuel (Sam) Chadwick, then principal of Cliff College, received a telephone call from someone seeking a preacher for the following Sunday's meeting.

"Well, you can have Mr. Jones," said Sam Chadwick. "But, if you have him, you'll have a revival."

"Oh, dear," said the startled voice at the end of the telephone. "We don't want *that*." And the line went dead.

As we trace the footsteps of this remarkable evangelist, from a gypsy tent across thousands of miles until the day of his death on board the *Queen Mary,* we might take heed. Those turnips could not say hallelujah, but we can!

2

Journey from the Forest

*I didn't go through your colleges and seminaries—
they wouldn't have me—but I have been to the feet
of Jesus where the only true scholarship is learned.*

Gipsy Smith often spoke about his life in the gypsy
tent. The story of his life made gripping hearing, and
he sometimes talked for two hours or more about the
way in which God had intervened in the life of a poor
gypsy lad. You can meet, even today, people who
heard that talk half a century ago—and they can
recite passages from it.

Gypsies, in our day, are a misunderstood minority.
The history of the gypsies, a fascinating subject itself,
shows that these mysterious people have sometimes
contributed to their poor reputation. But, as Gipsy
Smith himself said, they were often led astray by
gorgios (nongypsies) who attributed occult powers
to the Romanies.

"Every time one of you so-called Christians goes on
holiday, and there has his, or her, fortune told by a
gypsy, you lead a soul away from God!"

The Gipsy never spared words when it came to the
gypsies, whom he defended in print and from the

platform. A man of his calibre would undoubtedly help us to understand our generation of gypsies, who, in an increasingly conformist society, still choose to live on the fringe.

The evangelist was, of course, a real gypsy, born on the last day of March, 1860, in a gypsy tent pitched near Epping Forest to the east of London. His parents, Cornelius Smith and Mary (Polly) Welch, were both gypsies, and he was the fourth child, christened Rodney. The christening, Gipsy wryly remarks in his autobiography (from which subsequent quotes are taken), was a matter of good business. A gypsy christening always attracted the attention of gorgios, and they could hardly come without bringing gifts for the baby.

Britain was enjoying that all-too-brief period of mid-Victorian prosperity as the workshop of the world and ruler of a vast empire. Not that this had much effect on gypsy life. Cornelius made a living making and selling clothespins, baskets, and tin utensils. He was also a horse trader—this in fact was his specialty. Like so many other gypsies, he was Smith by name and by trade. Like many other gypsies too, Cornelius was a remarkable fiddler and, as we shall see, used to play his violin around the taverns.

These activities, which together made a way of earning a living, remind us of the very mystery of the gypsy race. Who are they? Where do they come from? Gypsies themselves have many traditions, for example, that they are descended from Judas Iscariot and are thereby cursed, or that their forebears made the nails by which Jesus was crucified, but only delivered three of the four. This tradition says that the gypsies are persecuted because the gorgios still search for the fourth nail. But these traditions only rationalize the sense of rejection experienced by so many of them. In fact, the origin of the gypsies has baffled the most astute scholars. Gipsy Smith, while maintaining that the gypsies were generally born into moral darkness, not least because of their inability to read and understand the Bible, added that they possessed an innate religious sense. Eighty out of every hundred gypsies own biblical names, he pointed out, and asked if this might not mean that the gypsies are one of the ten lost tribes? Observance of the Sabbath (i.e. Sunday) was, in his day, very strict among them, too. The marriage ceremonial was the same as that observed at the nuptials of Rebekah and Isaac. "Isaac brought Rebekah into his tent and she became his wife, and he lived with her."

Gypsy is not the correct name for the Romany race at all. This popular designation was derived from the belief that the gypsies came from "little Egypt." The word *Gypsy* (or *Gipsy*) came from the word *Egypt*. But they traveled a greater distance than that. Most scholars agree that the gypsies originated on the plains of central India, but, even then, they were a definite group. Their many traditions deserve study—for example, their preoccupation with cleanliness.

"Like the Jews," Gipsy Smith explained, "the gypsies are very clean. A man who does not keep his person or belongings clean is called 'chickly' (dirty) and is despised. They have hand towels for washing themselves, and these are used for nothing else. They are scrupulously careful about their food. They would not think of washing their tablecloth with the other linen. I saw my uncle trample on and destroy a copper kettle-lid because one of his children by mistake had dropped it in the washtub. It had become 'unclean.' "

In those comparatively unhurried days of Gipsy Smith's childhood, he enjoyed the joy of life in a close-knit family.

"The gypsy wagon," he said in later years, "can be the happiest home in the whole of England."

It certainly was for him, the most beautiful. The Smith family wandered through the rural counties of Essex, Suffolk, Norfolk, Cambridgeshire, Bedfordshire and Hertfordshire. The roads may not have been as wide as today's highways, but there was little traffic, and the knowledgeable gypsy could always find some secluded spot in which to rest.

Gipsy Smith claimed that he knew all the flowers of the field and trees of the forest, and even that he was followed home by the rabbits. Gypsies remain romantics to this day; one elderly gypsy claimed, in a recent radio program, that he used to play with the fairies when he was young—and he was quite certain about this!

We need not doubt Gipsy Smith's word, however, for in the best sense, he remained a child of nature all his life. The visiting preacher of our time rushes to the pulpit, without noticing the flowers on the piano or communion table. But the Gipsy would have paused and drawn the congregation's attention to the flowers. Like Jesus, he would have reminded his hearers that "even Solomon, in all his glory, was not arrayed as one of these."

We are all conscious of losing something as we grow up, leaving childhood behind us. That sense of loss came dramatically to the young Rodney, with the death of his mother from smallpox. Years later, as he told the story of his mother's death at public meetings, tears rolled down his face. This was no false emotion; even in middle age, with many years' labors yet before him, he said, "I often feel my hungry soul pining and yearning for my mother." But he could not remember what she looked like.

The story is simply told. The family was traveling in Hertfordshire, near a small village named Baldock, when the oldest child, a girl, was taken ill. The doctor did not enter the gypsy wagon, but simply walked up the steps and called the child to him for examination.

"She has smallpox!" he announced. "You must get out of the town at once."

The gypsy family was ordered to a lane, over a mile distant. It was there that Cornelius erected the tent. The four children free of the disease stayed there with their mother, while Cornelius took the wagon two hundred yards down the road, stopping it near an old chalk pit. From this point, Cornelius could see the tent clearly and could be called without difficulty. Cornelius looked after his sick daughter and, a few days later, his son, Ezekiel, who had also contracted the disease.

Gipsy's mother—still a young woman—used to walk up and down the lane, crying, "My poor children will die and I'm not allowed to look after them." She would go into Baldock to buy food and, after preparing it, take it down the lane toward the wagon. After going about half the distance, she would place the food on the ground and wave a silk handkerchief as a signal to Cornelius. Sometimes, he would come and collect the food at once, but this was not always possible. The inevitable happened: one day, Polly could keep away from her children no longer, and carried the food into the caravan where, caring for them, she caught the terrible disease. In a few days, she gave birth to the child she had been expecting, though the child outlived its mother by only a fortnight.

Cornelius was heartbroken when he knew that his wife was dying. One day, he asked her if she ever thought of God. When she replied that she had, he asked if she tried to pray.

"I try," she replied. "But a black hand comes before me and reminds me of all the wrongs I have done, and something says that there is no mercy for me."

Some short time before, Cornelius had been wrongly imprisoned for three months, and had there heard the gospel preached by a prison chaplain. So, as best he could, Cornelius related the story of Jesus to his wife, but he could not keep his feelings to himself and had to leave the wagon, weeping bitterly. Later, he was astonished to hear his wife gently singing an old chorus, "I have a Father in the promised land, and I must go to meet Him in the promised land." It was a chorus that she had heard many years before, as a little girl, at a Sunday school meeting.

"I am not afraid to die now," she told Cornelius. "I feel that it will be all right. I know that God will take care of you and the children."

It is not fashionable to show one's emotions now, and perhaps there is something sentimental in Gipsy Smith's memory of that sad day. Had that little boy but known it, God was in his infinite wisdom preparing him for an almost unimaginable work of blessing. Only a man who knows what it is like to lose all can identify himself with those who, not knowing Christ, are without hope.

We can imagine the Gipsy himself speaking to his congregations in much the same words as he wrote in 1901:

"I shall never forget that morning. I was only a little fellow, but even now I can close my eyes and see the gipsy tent and wagon in the lane. The fire is burning outside on the ground, and the kettle is hanging over it in true gipsy fashion. A bucket of water is standing nearby. Some clothes that my father had been washing are hanging on the hedge. I can see the old horse grazing along the lane. I can see the boughs bending in the breeze and I can almost hear the singing of the birds . . . and yet, when I try to call back the appearance of my dear mother, I am baffled. . . . I wandered up the lane that morning with the hand of my sister Tilly in mine. We two little things were inseparable. We could not go to our father, for he was too full of his grief. The others were sick. We two had gone off together, when suddenly I heard my name called: 'Rodney!' and running to see what I was wanted for, I encountered my sister Emily. She had got out of bed, and said to me, 'Rodney, mother's dead!' I remember falling on my face in the lane as though I had been shot, weeping my heart out, and saying to myself, 'I shall never be like other boys, for I have no mother!'"

The authorities would permit the funeral to be held only at night. Cornelius was the sole mourner, returning to the children just after midnight. Earlier in the day, their tent had caught fire, and most of their possessions had been destroyed; it was a dark day, indeed. And yet it was at this time that Gipsy Smith became conscious that he was a real boy. This was indeed the beginning of that journey from the forest and into the pulpit. It was an experience more significant than any member of that small, bereft family supposed.

3

Cornelius, a Tale Told in Silver

Drink is the devil in solution!

Someone once said that the story of Cornelius Smith ought to be written in silver. Gipsy Smith so loved his father that he often spoke about him. Indeed, at Torquay, Devon, at the end of one of his campaigns, Gipsy Smith was approached by one of the organizers and asked if his father would come and conduct a series of meetings. Subsequently, the aging but active Cornelius went to Torquay, and the good folk of that church expressed their sentiments thus: "We think we love the son [meaning Gipsy, of course] but we love the father more."

Cornelius was a true saint then but, at the time of his wife's death, he was just a lonely gypsy with the heavy responsibility of raising a young family. He possessed a superficial gaiety but this was not felt in his heart. He used to take his fiddle around the taverns at Baldock and thereabouts, playing to cheer the crowd, while young Rodney danced. Inevitably, the gypsy fiddler drank too much. Whenever Rodney saw that his father had drunk too much to know what he was doing, he would pass around the hat again—this time putting the proceeds into his own pocket.

As Gipsy Smith told his audiences around the world, "I reckoned myself a partner in the business, and not a sleeping partner at that!"

Rodney never drank, though he was often placed in the path of temptation. It is amazing to realize that, in all those evenings of dancing in the pubs of Hertfordshire, Rodney never took one glass of ale.

"The Lord saved me from all that!" he explained.

In one of his meetings, he claimed never to have touched a drop of alcoholic liquor in his entire life, whereupon his audience cheered.

"And neither have I smoked a cigarette!" he added. Then he observed that "not so many of you cheered that time!"

Cornelius was always ashamed of himself the following day, and prayed earnestly enough that he would not fall victim to drink again that evening. But, as soon as he became involved in the noise and bustle of the local inn, he took a glass and that was that. In his own way he was seeking salvation, but he was unable to read or write. Then, as now, people seemed more interested in moving gypsies away than in moving them on to salvation.

One day, near Luton, Bedfordshire, Cornelius and his little family were traveling in their wagon, when they saw two gypsy wagons coming toward them. Cornelius had paused to wait for his eldest daughter, who was selling her goods in the town. As the two wagons approached, Cornelius was overjoyed to see that they belonged to his two brothers, Woodlock and Bartholomew. What a reunion that was! The brothers had not met for some time; in fact, the others had not heard of the loss of Cornelius' wife. The children were taken into the wagons and comforted by the wives of the two brothers. As the three men—all of considerable stature physically, Cornelius being the eldest of the three and over six feet tall—sat on the bank, they discovered that Cornelius' search for God was shared by the other two. So they agreed to travel together for a while, not knowing that God was about to shape a journey together that would last their entire lives.

As they came into Cambridge, the city in which Gipsy Smith subsequently spent so many years, the three brothers paused at a beer-shop at the Barnwell end of the town. They began to talk to the landlady, and indicated their need for "the way that leads to peace of mind."

The woman recognized their need straight away and rushed upstairs to find a book which, as she said, "makes me cry whenever I read it."

The book was *The Pilgrim's Progress,* and a young man offered to read part of the story to the three large but illiterate men. At the point where Pilgrim loses his burden, Bartholomew jumped up and exclaimed, "That is what I need—my burden removed!"

Although the three brothers attended a service at the Primitive Methodist Chapel in Fitzroy Street, none of them was converted there. The minister undoubtedly challenged them, but they hesitated to come forward. In addition to the inner struggle that always comes on these occasions, the three men were gypsies, and had learned that gypsies were not always welcomed, even by the churches. So Cornelius left that meeting, his struggle unresolved.

They resumed their way to London and came to Epping Forest—not far from the spot where Gipsy

Smith had been born. Since it was too dark to proceed further, they made camp for the night. In true gypsy fashion, Cornelius placed his horse in a field for safety, intending to remove it early in the morning before the owner of the field discovered the trespass. During the night, Cornelius had a remarkable dream. It was as if Jesus Christ Himself came to Cornelius and showed him the marks of the nails in His hands. "I suffered all this for you, Cornelius. When you give up everything for Me and trust Me, I will save you."

He related his dream at breakfast, obviously affected by the experience. As he removed his horse from the field, he vowed "This will be the last known sin that I will ever commit." Cornelius was known by the other gypsies in the immediate locality, and he went to tell them that he was seeking God.

Gypsies believe in God, as we have seen, but often have a sense of guilt—not so much because some prey on the gorgios' gullibility (in fortune-telling, for example), but because of their folk myths. Many were moved by Cornelius' distress and, not for the first time, his own children wondered if their father might be losing his mind.

In company with his two brothers, Cornelius moved to Shepherds Bush on the outskirts of London where there were still a few fields in those days. The wagons were parked on a piece of building land, close to a chapel. Cornelius vowed that he would not move until his search for God had ended, and so he sold his horse. This was not only a truly remarkable step, but also a clear indication of his earnest intentions. How many of this generation would sell the family car in their search for God? But perhaps the analogy is faulty; a horse to a gypsy is, or was, more than a means of transportation; it was the very symbol of his wandering life.

God graciously led Cornelius to a roadmender who was a Christian. The two men entered into conversation, and the roadmender recognized the gypsy's need.

"You need converting," he said, "and there's a meeting this very night at the Latimer Road Mission Hall. You come along to that meeting and you'll be all right!"

The roadmender was a fairly astute fellow at that, because he called for Cornelius, who also brought his brother, Bartholomew.

"I will not come home again," Cornelius told his children, "until I am converted."

The children did not understand his words, and wondered if they might be losing their father. Perhaps this is why Rodney followed his father and Uncle Bartholomew into the crowded chapel. At this time, he was still called by his Christian name—almost forgotten in later life. As the people there sang the hymn, "There Is A Fountain Filled With Blood," Cornelius fell to the floor unconscious. Rodney, in great distress, thought that his father was dying, but the people at the mission hall had seen such agonies of spirit before and, ensuring that the gypsy was well, left him quietly on the floor.

Suddenly, Cornelius jumped to his feet exclaiming, "I am converted!" He kept looking at his flesh—it really seemed a different color. He felt, he said later, as if he could walk on eggs. Rodney did not wait to witness the rest of the meeting but rushed home, hardly knowing what had happened.

The children waited for Cornelius to return. The first thing they noticed was that his old haggard look had completely gone. There really was a new light about his face. He was as gentle as a child that night, gathering his family to him.

"Children," he said. "God has made a new man of me. You have a new father."

He was indeed a new man. He would look into the mirror, and ask, "Can this be old Cornelius?" Then he would burst into laughter and say, "Why, it is the *new* Cornelius!"

Bartholomew was also converted at that meeting, and brought his wife to Christ the same evening. Similarly, Cornelius used the first opportunity to preach Christ to the other gypsies camped on the same piece of land. The following morning, he and Bartholomew witnessed to them, and some fourteen gypsies were brought to Christ.

Woodlock was converted a little later and the three men made a vow never to separate again, but to be a source of strength one to another. They became evangelists—and you always had to take all three—as long as they were all alive. People who heard Cornelius recalled that his preaching was simple. He memorized large portions of Scripture and recited them with a personal testimony. Many were brought to Christ through that ministry. His qualities as a father were obvious. In 1904, for example, he conducted a campaign in Norfolk, and took a little girl upon his large knee.

"Well, my dear," he beamed, "you will love Jesus, won't you?" The beauty and inspiration of that encounter remains with that little girl, now a lady of many years, to this day.

A beautiful life lived for God is always its own testimony, even in a generation as sophisticated as our own. When Gipsy Smith found the rock of his message in the beauty of Jesus, he must have been thinking not only of his Heavenly Father, but of the godly father he knew on earth. When Cornelius and his brothers became converted, they decided to return to Baldock. It was there, you recall, that Cornelius used to play his fiddle and drink.

"We must go back and show them what God can do with a man's life," they decided.

They started back, though their journey must have been slow by today's standards for they held many evangelistic meetings by the roadside as they traveled. They stopped for the night just outside Melbourne, between Royston and Cambridge, and tethered the horses at the side of the road. At an early hour, they were aroused by a loud knock on the door of the wagon, and a demand to "open up." Four policemen were outside, empowered to arrest the three brothers supposedly for breaking a local ordinance. Because gypsies could be arrested without summons or warrant, the brothers were handcuffed and marched to the police station, a mile and a half away. It offered a good evangelistic meeting for the brothers, who witnessed of Christ every step of the way. In the cells they prayed and sang hymns. The policeman in charge of the cells was astonished, but, as Cornelius explained, the brothers were just following the good example of Paul and Silas (Acts 16). We cannot be sure if the policeman expected an earthquake to set his prisoners free; what is certain is that he brought them rugs to keep warm, while his wife brought hot coffee, bread, and butter. Cornelius gave her a tract, and she said that she would accept Christ as her Saviour. In the morning, the brothers were brought before the magistrates and fined twenty-five shillings. That was approximately $5.00, a considerable sum of money in those days. The alternative was fourteen days in prison. The brothers had no money, but the fines were paid. They never found out who paid them.

When Cornelius and his brothers arrived at Baldock they related the events of their evening in prison. People flocked to hear the three brothers and there were crowds outside a local tavern where, not so long before, Cornelius had played his fiddle while Rodney passed the hat. Another meeting, in a meadow, attracted so great a crowd that policemen were sent to keep order.

We shall be hearing more of Cornelius, who surely inspired so many of Gipsy Smith's actions.

They were on the same mental wavelength. Once, at a meeting at which Gipsy Smith had given an address, Cornelius grasped his son's arm and said, "I was in your waistcoat tonight, my boy." And Gipsy loved nothing more than to see his father after a meeting.

Cornelius lived until he was ninety-one, and was then laid to rest in Norton churchyard. Thousands knew God because of him. As for the evangelist himself, Gipsy Smith dedicated his autobiography to "My father, to whom, under God, I owe all that I am." Cornelius was never one to save the strap and spoil the child. In fact, in his childhood, Gipsy would do almost anything to avoid wrongdoing upon which his father, even in his unregenerate days, frowned. "You people like to run down the gypsies," Gipsy said to one crowd, "but you have never known them as I have. I tell you, my friends, I learned what the love of God was like at the knee of my father. He was never too tired or too busy to care for his children."

If he were alive today, he would surely add, "And no color television set makes up for a father's love."

4

Decision at Bedford

*The way to Jesus is not by Cambridge and Oxford,
Glasgow, Edinburgh, London, Princeton, Harvard,
Yale, Socrates, Plato, Shakespeare or the poets—it
is over an old-fashioned hill called Calvary.*

Rodney was one of six children. He had one brother
and four sisters. From the stories that he told of his
childhood one can only hope (for Cornelius' sake),
that the other children were not so mischievous! He
possessed, even as a child, the shrewdness characteristic of the gypsy trader. For example, when selling his
clothespins and tinware around the houses, he often
summed up the sales prospect at once. And, if the
sale was not going too well, Rodney would mention
that he was a child without a mother. Once, in Cambridge, he knocked at the door of a policeman's
house; being a mere ten years of age, he was charged
with selling goods without a license. But even in the
somewhat awesome surroundings of a court of law,
Rodney held his own. As he pointed out, he was only
trying to make an honest living. It was useless to talk
about gypsies stealing if you did not give them the
chance to live honestly, he added. He concluded his

case by saying that his father was certainly ready to pay for a trader's license, but implied that, whether this was permitted or not, he would continue to make an honest living. He was let off with a small fine, and there is little doubt that he left an abiding impression upon the court!

He must have looked every inch a child of nature in his "smockfrock," as he called it. This all-enveloping garment had many advantages, including very roomy pockets, which he loved to fill with various fruits of nature (you might say fruits of discovery). Once Rodney sat in a tree, enjoying some delicious Victoria plums. His pockets were full, of course, and the lad had a plum in his mouth. It probably had not occurred to him that someone owned the tree—that is, not until the owner appeared below and urged Rodney to come down. Rodney, seeing the stern look on the owner's face, declined the invitation but, as the owner replied grimly he would wait until nightfall if necessary, the lad slowly came down the tree.

The burly man pinched Rodney's ear and turned his head toward a notice which, though Rodney could not read it, boldly declared, "Whosoever is found trespassing on this ground will be prosecuted."

"Can you read that board, my boy?"

"No, sir."

"Then I will read it to you!"

The owner of the land very forcefully explained the meaning of the word *whosoever*. In one sense it was Rodney's first lesson in theology for, as he said, when the encounter was over he had no doubt at all as to the meaning of that word. The owner knew Cornelius, however, and would not prosecute. Even before the conversion of Cornelius Smith, people were inclined to treat him with respect—unusual for a gypsy. So Rodney escaped with his pockets full of plums, but he did not tell his father anything of the encounter. Had he done so there is little doubt that young Rodney would have had another lesson on the meaning of the law of trespass. Cornelius did not believe in sparing the rod and spoiling the child. Indeed, Rodney sometimes had the job of finding a stick for a due thrashing. Naturally, he tried to find sticks of modest size for the purpose! But Cornelius never struck the child in anger, and remember, he had five children to bring up.

The day came for Rodney to have his first pair of trousers. They were an old pair of his father's. To make them fit Rodney a simple expedient was found. The trousers were simply cut off at the knees; the result was a very baggy pair. Ezekiel, Rodney's brother, found a piece of string and, looking at the billowing trousers, asked what time the balloon went up. Rodney realized that his father secretly hoped that he would tire of the trousers and go back to the smock. He also knew that if he kept wearing the ridiculous trousers, sooner or later his father would buy him a new pair. The roomy trousers proved very useful. "Once," said Gipsy in his campaigns, "we were the guests of the Prince of Wales at Sandringham, one of the royal estates." In other words they pitched tents on his estate! Rodney managed to catch some rabbits and carried them home inside the trousers. "You see," smiled Gipsy, "how easily they became fur-lined trousers!"

Like most children, Rodney loved the circus. But money was very short in the Smith family, and Rodney resorted to the old trick of creeping in under the canvas. His sense of direction could not have been very good because he came out in the stables where the circus horses were kept. Before he could crawl back, Rodney encountered a policeman and, picking up a piece of harness nearby, began to polish it vigorously. The policeman thought that Rodney must be a member of the circus and stopped to talk with him.

"That's a funny job they've given you to do," he smiled.

"Oh, yes, and it is very hard work," replied Rodney, polishing harder than ever. He could not look into the policeman's face, for he knew that his looks would betray his guilt. At last, the policeman went and Rodney found his way into the circus tent. However, he found himself in the very best seats and could not enjoy the show for he believed that, at any moment, he would be recognized as an intruder. "There's only one way into heaven," he would add as he related this story later, "just as there was only one proper way into the circus. The only way into heaven is by the way of Jesus. Now, children, how many of you want to go to heaven by the good and proper way?"

They always responded to Gipsy's stories. As a boy, he was a handful; but, as he later pointed out, he was prevented from falling into serious sin by the limitations of his environment and by the watchfulness of his father. Without a doubt he would have something to say about the permissiveness afforded the children of our age.

"You say let them do what they like! But that's no way to bring up a child. He needs guidance and he needs security—and he can get neither unless he knows that the world is under the control of God. And, if you don't believe that this world is under the control of God, my friend, it's about time you lived in a gypsy tent for a month or two and found out what happens in nature. If there were no revival in nature, you'd get no spring potatoes."

Cornelius' conversion affected all the family, though it was some years before Lovinia—one of Rodney's sisters—was to come to Christ (and then at a Luton campaign conducted by her brother). Rodney became introspective and began to wonder if his life would be the wandering life of the gypsy, just going from place to place. In his middle teens he visited Bedford with his father. It was strange indeed that John Bunyan's work should again intervene in the affairs of the Smith family, for it was the reading of *Pilgrim's Progress* that started the brothers on their search. Now it was a visit to the home of John Bunyan that started Rodney on his. Rodney heard how John Bunyan had been a great sinner but had been converted and then had done a mighty work for God. As he stood at the foot of the statue of John Bunyan, Rodney decided he would live for God and go to meet his mother in heaven.

It was then that Rodney really started to become the evangelist who so shook England in later years, though he did not confess his new belief to anyone. That, he states in his autobiography, was a mistake. "If you follow Christ, tell others of your love for Him, for that is the way of strength and blessing."

A few days later, Cornelius and his family moved on to Cambridge, and it was here that Rodney publicly committed his life to Christ. He went to the small Primitive Methodist Chapel in Fitzroy Street. Although his life's decision had been made at Bedford, Rodney felt that he wanted to step out in front of the congregation. In those days—less than a century ago, but so far away in much of our present-day experience—churches *expected* decisions for Christ to be made in the normal course of the meeting. There was more emotion in those meetings than in ours but that might have been their gain. Certainly, the evangelist always looked back at that meeting with great tenderness and affection. During the singing of a gospel hymn, Rodney went forward and knelt at the communion rail, on the invitation of the minister, the Reverend George Warner. As he knelt, he heard someone whisper, "Oh, it's *only* a gypsy boy." But he had a great-hearted counselor in the person of an elderly man with an abundance of white hair.

"You know what you are doing?" the counselor smiled. "It is a great step to take, giving one's life to Jesus."

"Well," replied Rodney, "I cannot trust myself for I am nothing. I cannot trust in what I have for I have nothing; and I cannot trust in what I know for I know nothing. It won't be hard for me to trust Jesus."

Rodney rushed home after the meeting to tell his father the news. Cornelius was overjoyed, but he wanted to make sure.

"How do you know that you are converted?" he asked of his son.

"Because I feel so warm in my heart," Rodney replied.

The date was November 17, 1876.

On the following day Rodney set out with his goods as usual. He had to learn the lesson that conversion does not instantly solve the problems of living in this world, though it lifts the soul to a new dimension. Before he started selling his wares Rodney decided to go and look at the chapel where, only hours before, he had taken that momentous step. As he gazed at the building he heard a shuffling of feet and turned to see his counselor, the old man, coming towards him. At first Rodney was overjoyed, then—from his gypsy experience— froze into stillness. "Now the old man will see that I am just a gypsy boy selling clothespins," he reasoned, "he will not stop to speak to me." But the old man did more than that. Despite the fact he could walk only with the aid of canes, he came over to Rodney and gave him his blessing, just a few simple words before he turned and walked away.

"The Lord bless you, my boy. The Lord keep you."

Rodney was too moved to reply. The old man turned the corner and Rodney never saw him again. Later, when Rodney had achieved that status of world-famous evangelist, he was often called upon to narrate the events of his conversion. He always mentioned the old man.

"Indeed," he would say, "I might not be here tonight but for him. Many converts fall away and are lost to the church for want of a simple kindness like that shown by the old man. When I get to heaven, and all those souls brought to Christ at our meetings cry for joy, I will thank that old saint from the bottom of my heart."

Rodney's conversion opened his mind in a remarkable way. He developed a great desire to learn. In one sense his direction had been established; his education was now to begin.

Of course Rodney, at sixteen, knew more of the ways of nature than many would acquire in a lifetime. And, as a salesman, he knew a few tricks plucked from his observation of human nature. But this new awakening was for book-learning. He acquired three large books—the Bible, an English dictionary and a Bible dictionary—and carried them everywhere, much to the amusement of his family.

"Never you mind," Rodney said. "One day, I'll be able to read them." Then he added, "And I'm going to preach, too."

5

A Field Full of Turnips

I see God in the opening of the gates of the morning without a creak on their hinges.

Rodney's childhood ambition was to be a circus barker or what he called a "pinafore billy." This was the man who would stand outside the circus tent and relate the delights of the show within, so that people would pay and come inside. Rodney, with his natural enthusiasm and flair for salesmanship, would have been very successful in this line of business. But his powers of oratory were to have a quite different audience.

Cornelius was certainly an example to the boy. With Woodlock and Bartholomew he rejoiced to preach to the gypsies, and anyone else that came along, even though opposition was often vociferous and sometimes involved acts of physical violence. Fortunately, the three brothers were big men and able to look after themselves. As Cornelius surely pointed out, "Who has a greater champion than us, or One better able to protect?"

It is interesting to recall that, within a few weeks of their conversion, the three gypsy brothers walked all the way from Shepherds Bush to Loughton in Essex (a distance of some twenty miles) to witness to their parents. As they approached, the gypsy trio burst into song, "Gentle Jesus, meek and mild." Their parents, both seventy years of age, were amazed and delighted, though Cornelius' father reproached himself: "My boys have come home to teach me what I should have told them." Cornelius called the family to prayer before they shared that memorable meal, and his father prayed for forgiveness. Indeed, Cornelius' uncle, only one year from his hundredth birthday, was converted, too.

During the summers of 1873-1875, the three brothers held many evangelistic meetings as they traveled around Cambridge and the counties east of London. Gypsy children rarely enjoyed the advantages of an education. However, Gipsy Smith used to say at his missions, "I come from Cambridge, so I call myself a Cambridge man."

Cornelius used his musical talents to good effect. He now played what was called "the hallelujah fiddle" to attract attention—and a crowd. The three brothers, with all the children of the three families, would sing until a crowd had gathered (sometimes as many as three or four hundred people). Then Cornelius and his brothers would preach. Of course, the approach was simple. The men knew little theology, but the Holy Spirit radiated love through the lives of these consecrated men.

The impact of these meetings was considerable, and at Forest Gate in London revival was enjoyed to the extent that a mission hall was built. During this period the brothers came into contact with the Reverend (later General) William Booth who, characteristically, gave them some sound advice.

"The way to keep bright and happy," Mr. Booth

told them, "is to work for God. And the best way to work for God is to take Christ to the people who don't know Him."

So confident was Mr. Booth in the powers of the three gypsy brothers that he invited them to take a week's series of meetings in Portsmouth. The brothers were away, not for one week but for six, as the work flourished. Naturally it was hard on the children, and in his talks about his childhood, Gipsy Smith often spoke about the day that Cornelius finally came home.

"We waited all day, expecting him—as children would—to come in the morning. But he didn't get home until six in the evening. As was our custom we made way for the baby of the family, Tilly, to get the father's embrace first. But she stayed such a long time in my father's arms that I became impatient and told her it was my turn. Tilly cheerfully said that I was welcome if I could get her out. 'Never mind,' I said. 'I'm coming in, too.' And I did! You know, there is room in our heavenly Father's arms for everyone, and no one can ever take us away."

So Rodney had plenty of opportunity to hear effective preaching. It was not learned preaching, but then the test of preaching is its effect in bringing people to Christ and in deepening the spiritual experience of Christians. There were no college diplomas in the gypsy wagons but the Lord was surely in their midst. Just as William Booth played an important part in the work of Cornelius, so he was to call Rodney to the preaching ministry.

But, first of all, Rodney had to pursue a certain amount of self-education. He took his three books almost everywhere. Whenever he came across a word he did not know, he turned to the dictionary at once. This was a practice he followed for many years. Sometimes he had to use a Romany word to fully express himself. For example, years later during a meeting at Bath (where his son, Hanley, was a Methodist minister), the evangelist said, "It isn't what you intend to do that counts, it's the little bit extra you put into the job. It's what we gypsies call the *brota.*" That was just the kind of thought that remained in the listener's mind, long years later.

Rodney, just sixteen, began to practice preaching. One Sunday he went into a turnip field and preached to the turnips, a "very large and attentive congregation." As he walked along the road with the basket of clothespins and tinware under his arm, he would go on preaching, linking together passages of Scripture and hymns. One Christian gentleman, overhearing young Rodney, told Cornelius that the boy ought to go to Mr. Spurgeon's college, but that never came about. The basis for his lifelong skill as a personal evangelist was shaped at this time for, after having sold some clothespins (or even if he had failed to do so) Rodney would sing hymns to the people he met, sometimes in a kitchen or even at the door. He came to be known as "the singing gypsy boy" and was often asked to come into the homes to speak to housemeetings. These gatherings may have been somewhat spontaneous, but they proved of great value. As Rodney's ability to read grew, he learned portions of Scripture by heart—the fifty-third and fifty-fifth chapters of Isaiah and the fifteenth chapter of St. Luke.

His spiritual life deepened considerably. One day he took shelter in a half-finished building during a sudden rainstorm. He decided to spend some time in prayer and knelt down among the shavings and the sawdust. After praying aloud for some little time, he heard a sob and, looking up, saw he had an audience. Three men, their caps removed, were looking through the window. They had obviously been deeply moved by the boy's prayers. Startled, Rodney took up his basket and his cap and ran out into the rain.

Rodney's seventeenth birthday came and, with it, his desire to be a preacher grew. One Sunday morning he decided it was time to take a stand. So, in his Sunday clothes, he went forth for his public preaching debut. It was in the open air, and the Sunday clothes were better fitted for that, than for the Victorian pulpit. He wore a small brown beaver hat, a velvet jacket with white pearl buttons, a matching waistcoat, a pair of corduroy trousers and a yellow and red handkerchief around his neck.

Standing in a small corner some distance from the gypsy wagons, Rodney knew that the people would have to pass that way as they went to church. As they approached, Rodney started to sing some hymns and to say some brief prayers. When he had gained the attention of a fairly substantial group of people, Rodney gave a brief testimony. He told them why he loved Jesus and why they should. But, like many a preacher since, Rodney was not quite sure how to finish. However, he concluded by telling the people that he hoped to do better next time—and then crept back to the wagons. He did not feel particularly exultant, but his father gave words of encouragement.

It was on Whitmonday (Monday after Pentecost), 1877, that **Rodney** took that first step which took him into the pulpits of the world. With his father and other members of the Smith family he went to an all-day meeting held by the Reverend William Booth at his mission's headquarters in Whitechapel Road, London. William Booth, always a very observant man, noticed the gypsies almost immediately and realized that Rodney must be the embryonic evangelist. So after various people had spoken, Mr. Booth smiled and announced: "Our next speaker will be the gypsy boy."

Rodney's first inclination was to depart, but he realized this was impossible so, with trembling limbs, he went onto the platform. It was at that meeting he sang his first solo in public. After this, Rodney cleared his throat before giving his short word. A tall man nearby called out, "Keep your heart up, youngster!"

"My heart is in my mouth already," Rodney replied, "Where do you want it?"

This was quite a spontaneous reply, and Rodney did not intend the remark to be heard. It was, however, and the laughter relieved the tension that the boy had felt. He went on to give a short testimony which was well received.

Gipsy Smith always carried a pocketful of laughter around with him. He did not try to be funny—nothing is worse than forced joviality when one is about the Lord's business—but there was a simple touch of sunshine in his ministry. Many years after his greatest campaigns people still remember the laughter they enjoyed at one or other of his stories, or at one of his spontaneous comments.

Mr. Booth took the boy aside after the meeting. "If there is rejoicing in heaven, there is surely laughter, too" were the sentiments of Mr. Booth, who saw that

there were untapped depths in the somewhat nervous
gypsy boy who had made the people smile—and also
made them think.

"Will you leave everything and come and be an
evangelist in the Christian Mission?" Mr. Booth asked
him. The minister made sure that Rodney understood
what the cost would be: to say goodbye to his home
and family, and to accept a task as hard as any that
could be found in the kingdom. Rodney told Mr.
Booth that if the minister believed him fitted for the
job he would take it as an answer to prayer. So the
date for Rodney's new work was fixed as the twenty-
fifth of June.

Naturally, Rodney was excited when he came home.
He took his three books and marched in front of the
wagon.

"Rodney is going to be a great preacher," his
brother said.

It was innocent enthusiasm, and there was nothing
wrong with the sense of achievement at being called
to preach. "You ministers look as though you're full
of apologies," Gipsy Smith said to a group of pastors.
"Don't you know you've got the most important job
in the world?"

So young Rodney was taking on the most important
job in the world. It was a day or so before he realized
that the small brown beaver hat, the velvet jacket and
the yellow and red handkerchief would have to be
discarded in favor of attire more suitable for a young
evangelist.

6

Stone Walls

It is a brave thing when a man makes up his mind to serve God. It is not a weak thing—you think it is? It is not a childish thing—it may be a childlike thing.

"I want a frock coat, a waistcoat and a pair of striped trousers," Rodney announced to the somewhat startled counter clerk. He had counted his savings carefully and estimated he had more than enough for a good "preacher's suit." The clerk found the correct sizes for the gypsy lad and carefully parceled them. But when he went to push the parcel across the counter, Rodney ordered, "Send them, please. Do you know that I am going to be a preacher?" It must have been one of the very few occasions upon which the clerk delivered such formal attire to a gypsy tent!

The twenty-fifth of June came soon enough and Rodney put on the splendid suit. He was the object of much admiration by his sisters and, one suspects, a little hilarity, because Rodney was plainly uncomfortable. Half in jest they called Rodney a Romany Rye (a gypsy gentleman) and *Boro Rashie* (a great preacher). Little did they realize they were speaking prophetically. Rodney had found an adequate box for his clothing and other items needed for his new life, and two cousins carried it to Forest Gate Railway Station. It seemed to be something of a small procession for, as Gipsy pointed out when telling the story, the box was not heavy and was really too large for his modest possessions. However the occasion demanded a big box— so there it was!

At Aldgate Rodney was met by one of Mr. Booth's missionaries, a godly man named Bennett. Rodney was taken to his lodgings, quite near the mission's headquarters, and his hosts gave him a warm welcome. For the very first time in his life Rodney was faced with the challenge of a table setting. Handling the knife and fork was difficult enough, but he was very much puzzled by the table napkin and concluded that his hosts had provided him with a free pocket handkerchief, in case he did not have one of his own. It must have been difficult for his hosts to repress their smiles, but they did so admirably. Rodney apologized for his lack of knowledge of etiquette, and this was accepted with understanding.

Following the meal Rodney was shown to his apartment. The word was unfamiliar to him but that was no time to find his dictionary and look it up. His apartment was comfortable enough but, to Rodney, it seemed like prison. When the door was closed on him, Rodney's heart sank. He felt suffocated. Then, recovering himself, he inspected his surroundings. The bed, to Rodney's eye, appeared fragile and he made quite sure that it would hold his weight. He decided it was time to sleep and, after undressing, took a running leap into bed. It was a feather bed, but the feathers hitherto known to Rodney were those in the fields, and so he slept fitfully, dreaming of his family and the gypsy wagon that now seemed so far away. He rose early and prayed that God would help him to tackle the new work given to him. The room did not flood with light but Rodney felt comforted and, although he had now to tackle the problems of using a washbowl and hand towel for the first time, he enjoyed a renewed sense of God's purpose in his life.

Those first few weeks in London held many problems for young Rodney, enough to discourage many Christians, but he persevered. There was, for example, the problem of reading the portion of Scripture at the meetings. Rodney was not a good reader by any means and wondered if he ought to ask someone to read the lesson for him. He dismissed this thought, however, for it would never do to show inability to read one's own selected part of Scripture. So he adopted a course which stood him in good stead for some considerable time: whenever he read a passage from the Bible, he continued until he came to a word that he could not pronounce or understand. Then he would stop just before that problematical word, address a few remarks to his audience bearing upon what he had just read, and then continue reading from the other side of the difficult word.

Some people might have objected had they recognized Rodney's plan but, although life at William Booth's mission was hard, it was also godly. Even if Rodney was later dismissed from the Salvation Army, on a matter which now seems fairly trivial, Mr. Booth was largely responsible for the making of this evangelist. God honored the boy's work, too. His meetings were crowded and greatly blessed.

To Rodney's delight, his youngest sister, Tilly, was converted at one of his meetings. It happened while he was singing, and the occasion was a special blessing because Rodney had once believed that he stood in the way of Tilly's conversion. The children had been converted in order of age and Rodney, being older than Tilly, had believed that she could not come to the Lord until he had. And, as we know, Rodney had quite a struggle in making his decision.

Gradually he became used to the starched collar. Indeed, during the whole of his long life, Gipsy Smith was always immaculately dressed. But the starched collar never produced starched sermons. "I will be stiff long enough when I am dead," he would say when people asked him why he took such a natural, spontaneous approach to his work.

At the age of eighteen Gipsy Smith went to Whitby, a fishing port in Yorkshire. Delayed by indifferent railway connections, he spent nine hours on the platform at York, without money or food. It seemed to be just the occasion for impromptu evangelism and it is likely that the railway porters to whom he spoke (along with other waiting travelers) were relieved to see the earnest young Salvationist depart on the 5 A.M. train!

The Gipsy arrived at his host's home just after nine o'clock, very ready for breakfast. His host was "Fiery Elijah" Cadman, one of the most amazing converts that the Salvation Army ever had. Formerly a pugilist and street tough, Elijah was converted as a teenager shortly after witnessing a public hanging—a grisly scene that prompted him to ponder on his way of life. "Fiery Elijah" gave the Gipsy breakfast and then told him that there were four meetings to attend that day.

The fishermen enjoyed the Gipsy's singing and he soon began to attract the crowds. He also attracted the eye of a young lady, some two years his senior. Annie Pennock was the daughter of a ship's captain and it was not long before she and the evangelist became engaged. Since "Fiery Elijah" did not believe in mixing soul-winning with romance, he wrote to William Booth. In the Gipsy's words, "I was removed from the town." However, he returned to marry Annie in December, 1879, by which time he had already disagreed with his superiors on at least one other occasion, a portent of the inevitable parting of the ways.

The Gipsy's first assignment as a married man was at Chatham in Kent. A somewhat divided congregation of thirteen gave him a frigid reception, and a spokesman finally told the evangelist that he was too young.

"I may not have any more whiskers on my face than a gooseberry!" the Gipsy retorted. "But I'm old enough to have a wife!"

They gave him a chance. In nine months the congregation had grown to two hundred and fifty persons.

The Gipsy learned soon enough that the barriers he had to face were those of stony hearts rather than stone walls.

7

Revival at the Ice House

One of the greatest privileges and honors of the Christian is the joy of witnessing that He saves to the uttermost.

The six months Rodney Smith spent in Hull, another Yorkshire seaport, during 1881, were among the happiest in his entire life. Strange indeed that so warm a personality should have found himself in charge of the Ice House! This was the second of the Salvation Army strongholds in Hull and was strategically situated on the main Anlaby Road. Rodney was present at the opening ceremony, accompanying the energetic General who was a little perturbed that a £1,000* debt was still outstanding on the building. Not that William Booth had any doubt that it would be found. "My principle of bookkeeping is the most sound on earth," he declared. "It goes by the name of faith and can be summed up in the words, 'The Lord will provide.'" There were very strict rules about the use of money in the Salvation Army and, as we shall see later, an in-

*At the time, the British pound sterling was equivalent to approximately four dollars.

nocent gift was responsible for Rodney's departure from
that energetic company. But that was still in the
future on that happy day in Hull.

A Mr. Denny offered to donate £200 toward the
cost of the Ice House if the people together raised
the remaining £800. This handsome gesture aroused
the enthusiasm of some local Army members and they
told General Booth that, if Captain Rodney Smith
could take over the work, the sum would soon be
raised. One wonders if the General, who had so many
responsibilities, hesitated before he agreed. Many a
fine young evangelist had succumbed to the greatest,
and perhaps least obvious, temptation of all, the slow
but sure growth of self-importance.

By this time the public and press had begun calling
him Gipsy Smith, and so he adopted the name. At the
beginning of the work he had been advertised as "Rodney Smith, the gipsy boy." His father, Cornelius, and
uncles, Woodlock and Bartholomew, were known as
"The Three Converted Gypsies." It all made for a
certain confusion so Rodney decided to become, quite
simply, Gipsy Smith. But alas, this confusion was
never completely put to rest. A "Gipsy Simon Smith"
used to conduct evangelical campaigns in Wales and,
to this day, many gypsies engaged in evangelism have
adopted the obvious prefix to their names.

Gipsy Simon Smith was, in fact, first cousin to
Rodney, and the son of Bartholomew. He died only a
few years before the subject of our book. When Rodney's mother died, Simon's mother cared for him and
was undoubtedly a great force for good in his life.
Like his cousin, Gipsy Simon Smith possessed a fine
singing voice, which he used to good effect in his

campaigns; and both men shared a certain genius in composing memorable religious songs or hymns. At the present time, Gipsy Simon Smith is perhaps better remembered in Canada and the USA, where he conducted countless campaigns, than in Britain (though he certainly attracted crowds at campaigns held in London, for example, and was presented to the late King George V and Queen Mary.) Both gypsy evangelists appeared together in the pulpit of the Metropolitan Church in Toronto.

The name Gipsy Smith gained a gradual predominance over Captain Rodney Smith, though some people simply called him the Gipsy. Gipsy (for such we will call him from now on), was not too concerned with the name above the door. "I'm not interested in your denomination, my friend. It's your destination I'm concerned with!"

The meetings at the Ice House were crowded, if that modest word can describe the enormous crowds that flocked to hear the evangelist. At times the building would be full and the crowds overflowing onto the street outside. Characteristically Gipsy would hold a spontaneous open-air meeting for the people who could not get in. There were many decisions for Christ. It was not unusual, Gipsy recalled, to have a meeting of a thousand people who had been converted at his meetings. What was even more amazing was the renewal of the prayer life of the people. As many as fifteen hundred people would come to the prayer meeting early Sunday morning. Some of the converts were hard cases, people who had been on the wrong side of the tracks and had stayed there. Gipsy was, in some strange way, able to reach the people to whom organized religion meant nothing and who had been largely forgotten by the churches.

"I can tell you something about those wonderful times at the Ice House," Gipsy would recall during one of his meetings. "We needed two policemen at every service to manage the crowds at the doors. I always hoped the sergeant would send two different policemen every night so that they'd all hear the gospel!"

The revival at the Ice House also aided the cause of religious publications and together with the smaller work at Sculcotes, a nearby village, fifteen thousand copies of *The War Cry* were sold every week.

One of Gipsy's friends and colleagues at the Ice House was a Lieutenant Evens and, in 1883, he was married to Tilly, Gipsy's youngest sister. During the following year George Bramwell Evens was born at 3 Argyll Street, Anlaby Road, and grew up to be a preacher almost as remarkable as his Uncle Rodney. As a Methodist minister, George Bramwell Evens shared the same love of nature as Gipsy Smith, and started broadcasting as "Romany" in the Children's Hour radio programs, "Romany and Raq." He was a superb artist and wrote several books. Hull can be proud indeed that such a godly man came from its precincts.

From the glory of the Ice House, Gipsy went to the defeats of Derby, an industrial town in the Midlands. The work there was a partial failure and Gipsy found himself unable to get on with members of the local corps, whom he accused of worldliness. Most prophets discover that there are valleys in every human experience; it is a necessary lesson, though we do not care for the tuition. General Booth raised no objection when Gipsy expressed his wish to leave Derby.

"Well, where do you want to go next?" the General inquired.

"Send me to the nearest place to the bottomless pit," Gipsy retorted.

So the General sent him to Hanley in Staffordshire. With his wife and firstborn son Albany, Gipsy arrived in the town on the last day of December, 1881. It did not appear a promising prospect at all. The smoke from the potteries and the smell of sulphur from the iron foundries made Gipsy think the General had taken him at his word almost too literally!

Taking a horse-drawn taxi at Hanley station, Gipsy searched the town for lodgings. As soon as he mentioned he was in the Salvation Army, however, prospective landladies immediately lost interest and slammed their front doors. It was not popular to be in the Army, and it appeared to be even less so to give lodgings to its officers. Finally Gipsy found accommodation in a humble but adequate home of a poor Welsh lady. No doubt Gipsy later sang to her to express his gratitude!

After ensuring that his wife and child were settled, Gipsy went to examine the "battlefield." Two or three weeks earlier, three young men had been dispatched to Hanley to start Salvation Army meetings, which were held in the old Batty Circus. This was the most uncomfortable and depressing place that the Gipsy had ever seen. The ring of the circus had been left just as it was when the circus people had left—knee-deep in sawdust and dirt. On that memorable Saturday evening, New Year's Eve, Gipsy entered as a small group of people, perched about the circus ring in uncomfortable seats, sang "I need Thee, Oh! I need Thee." Gipsy just stood and laughed. "Well," he said. "They need somebody."

The three young lieutenants stood in the ring, using it as a pulpit. Gipsy joined them and said a few words to the people. "Meet me in the market place tomorrow morning at ten o'clock," he invited them. But none of the congregation turned up. Two young lieutenants with the Gipsy and his wife sang hymns, aided by a concertina which had been presented to the Gipsy by some friends in Devonport. The open-air meeting was certainly *not* the most successful in the Gipsy's career. One or two people thought the group were out-of-work laborers and threw a few pennies in their direction.

The Gipsy was not then wearing the Army uniform (in fact, he never wore a red jersey in his entire life). Instead he was dressed in gypsy clothing. One can imagine the good General snorting "How can a man be in the Army if he doesn't wear the uniform?" Perhaps, subconsciously, the Gipsy already saw a mission wider than even the Salvation Army itself.

On one Sunday evening at the beginning of January, 1882, about eighty people turned up at the Batty Circus—a significant increase in the congregation, but hardly one to make the meetings any more successful. The barnlike building seated two and a half thousand, and the eighty people huddled together in an attempt to keep warm, physically and spiritually. It was, as Gipsy confessed, "a dismal beginning." However he was the kind of man who recognized problems as the reverse side of opportunities; and, on the fol-

lowing day, he returned to the Batty Circus to make a
thorough tour of inspection. There were windows to
repair, cracks in the doors, and drafts galore. The
Gipsy and his friends found some timber in the stable
and immediately set to work. His wife held a candle
for Gipsy as he ventured into the darker corners of the
building. Being the wife of an evangelist was not, then
as now, as glamorous as people sometimes thought.
For about a fortnight the stalwarts hammered and
banged away. Seats were made for the ring and the
building was made a little more respectable and welcoming. In the meantime the open-air meetings in the
market place continued. The audience grew with every
one. The Gipsy had a remarkably good singing voice
and needed no artificial aids for amplification. When
he sang, one would have to be hard of hearing indeed
not to hear him, and very hard spiritually not to understand his message. But although much good work
was done in the market place, few people came to the
Batty Circus. Perhaps this should teach us, in our
times, that people's receptivity to the gospel is not
necessarily measured by their readiness to come to our
churches.

The first month's collections covered the gas bill,
but nothing more. There was no money for the rent
and no money for the support of evangelists. Every
Salvation Army station had to be self-supporting, a
principle with which the Gipsy heartily agreed, so he
could hardly apply for financial help. However the
General did the struggling soldiers in Hanley an im-
measurably good turn by giving them the services of
the Fry family, a father and three sons who really
started the musical traditions of the modern Salvation

Army. The Fry family, as you can read in any popular
history of the Army, were enthusiastic musicians who
decided to use their talents in an endeavor to overcome local opposition to their cause. Despite some
danger to their own well-being (and their instruments!)
the Fry family used to escort the local brigade by
playing popular hymn tunes and marches. It certainly
gave new heart to the soldiers. Although the Fry family
could work with the Gipsy for only a few days, he
decided to make the most of this splendid opportunity.

"First of all we need someone of good local reputation to preside at our meeting," Gipsy told his
colleagues.

The name of Alderman Boulton, the Mayor of
Burslem, was proposed and fortunately, the Reverend
John Gould, then Wesleyan minister at Hull, had already told the alderman of the great work done at the
Ice House. So the alderman accepted the invitation
when it came. In addition he invited many of his
friends to come to the meeting too. In fact, when the
meeting started the platform was quite full of local
dignitaries and there was a great sense of expectancy
in the air. The alderman, to his credit, avoided the
limelight and simply introduced the Gipsy by referring
to the blessings experienced at Hull.

"We all want to hear the Gipsy," he said. "So I
will not take up any more time."

Happy is the man who knows when to step aside!
There was a large audience but the Gipsy kept his
sermon short, working on the principle of getting
them to return to hear more. The singing led by the
Fry family was terrific, almost raising the roof of that
large, echoing building. We hear no more about the

Mayor of Burslem, Alderman Boulton, in the work at Hanley but he, as much as anybody could, gave an impetus that sent the message rolling on.

This station, "the nearest place to the bottomless pit," experienced a great spiritual revival in the following months. What had seemed the most unpromising of places turned out to be one of the milestones in the Gipsy's life. As he so often said, "Where it's hardest, there's often the harvest."

8

Dismissal

*You may know all the organization of the church;
you may know the letter of the law as well as you
know your own name, but you may know nothing of
vital godliness.*

In one sense it was inevitable. Gipsy Smith was an
individualist, the kind of man who finds it hard to
fit into any organization. Before we pass any judgment
upon him we might well remember that Elijah would
not necessarily be the ideal Methodist, or Peter the
perfect Congregationalist. We have always to remember that our denominations are to be the servants of
that greatest of all causes, the proclamation of the
kingdom of God.

By the end of June, 1882, Gipsy Smith had made a
considerable impression upon Hanley. Annie, his wife,
was not very well, however, and when General Booth
informed the young captain it was time for him to
move on, a mild uproar broke out among local Christians. They did not want to see their leader go so soon;
and, as they argued, it would be wise for Gipsy to
stay in Hanley until his wife was a little better. This
request, put to the General, met with his approval; but

it seems certain that he must have been concerned at the personal following the captain now possessed. General Booth had no time for what some call "the cult of personality." To help Gipsy Smith in his extended work in Hanley, a committee of local Protestant churches was formed; and in July, 1882, they gave the evangelist a suitably inscribed gold watch. The sum of five pounds (about $20.) was given to Gipsy's wife and a similar sum to his sister, Tilly. A wonderful sense of fellowship was experienced at the public meeting arranged for the presentation of these gifts and Gipsy, a modest man at heart, was visibly affected by the sentiments of his friends.

"Whatever good work has been achieved at Hanley," he said, "is that of the Lord, not of any man."

He could not have suspected the reaction from the Army's hierarchy. The soldiers of the Salvation Army had not been involved in the presentation: they had indeed planned some gift, but Gipsy discouraged them. About a fortnight after the presentation Major Fawcett, Gipsy's superior officer, called and made what appears to have been an official investigation into the nature of the gifts. Gipsy rightly pointed out they were no more than a modest expression of the gratitude of local Christians and that the Army might well be pleased at the sign of goodwill. He added that other officers had received similar, modest gifts—including one in Birmingham who, only a fortnight earlier, had been given a silver watch. Major Fawcett made notes and said the Gipsy would be hearing from headquarters in due course.

On August 4, a telegram arrived for the two lieuten-

ants working under Gipsy Smith. This summoned them
to London at once and Gipsy urged them to obey the
command promptly. There was no message for the
Gipsy himself although, by this time, he had been in
the Army for five years. The lieutenants, in contrast,
had a mere six months' service. On arrival at the
Training Home in Clapton, London, the lieutenants
were threatened with dismissal if they did not give up
their watches at once. Early the following morning, a
Saturday, Gipsy's second child, a son, Hanley, was
born. A few hours after the happy event, the anticipated letter came. Bramwell Booth wrote tersely enough
but Gipsy could hardly believe his eyes. He read the
letter once, then twice, then three times. It was very
final:

"We understand that on Monday, July 31st, a presentation of a gold watch was made to you at Hanley,
accompanied by a purse containing £5 for your wife.
We can only conclude that this has been done in pre-
meditated defiance of the rules and regulations of
the Army to which you have repeatedly given your
adherence and that you have fully resolved no longer
to continue with us. The effect of your conduct is already seen to have led younger officers under your
command also astray.

"Having chosen to set the General's wishes at defiance, and also to do so in the most public manner
possible, we can only conclude that you have resolved
to leave the Army. Anyhow, it is clear that neither
you nor your sister can work in it any longer as officers, and the General directs me to say that we have
arranged for the appointment of officers to succeed you
at Hanley at once."

Gipsy Smith's life had always been eventful, but instant dismissal, following upon his new family responsibilities so quickly, greatly upset the young evangelist. The letter—as we read it today—was uncharitable and, as the Gipsy pointed out, inaccurate. He certainly had not led his two lieutenants astray. As far as Gipsy Smith had known, the prohibition on gifts applied only to presents from other Army officers (a sentiment with which he entirely agreed, knowing the financial hardship of men enlisted in the Army). It seems obvious that the presentation was the inevitable point of departure which the General had anticipated for a long time. He was an autocrat—a godly autocrat and a great Christian—but an autocrat all the same. The Army just wasn't big enough for the General *and* Gipsy Smith—at that time, anyway.

But then we have to remember the heavy responsibilities that rested upon the General's shoulders. Maybe he saw that Gipsy's ministry would go further outside the Army. At heart, the General only did what he considered best for the Salvation Army. Gipsy Smith certainly admits that by this time he did not like the uniform or the regulations of the Army. His style was Salvationist in the most honorable sense of that word but, as a soldier, he made a good candidate for the awkward squad.

Few Christians take unjustified criticism well. In that we have so much to learn from our Lord Jesus Christ. Gipsy's first thought was to take the letter to the local newspaper and to reply to Bramwell's comments in public. Then he reflected that such a course could only cause problems to the work of evangelism in the Batty Circus. So he kept the matter to himself

until the close of the evening service, when he read
the letter aloud. Although the building was crowded,
the congregation heard the Gipsy in complete silence—
and amazement. As the letter was read, some of the
people began to hiss.

"That is not Christianity," said the Gipsy. "We have
preached charity. Now we have to practice it."

The crowd dispersed quietly but was still aroused
emotionally. Gipsy wrote to Bramwell Booth in a firm
but courteous manner. He must have realized that
nothing he could say would make any difference. "I
can hold the world at defiance as regards my moral
and religious life. If I leave you, I do so with a clear
conscience and a clean heart."

During the following days many meetings were held
and various letters written to General Booth. It was
arranged that he would reconsider the matter and
telegraph his decision on Thursday. The telegram
came: "Dismissal must take its course." The General
could really do nothing else.

Gipsy Smith was the most popular man in Hanley.
At the close of his last service as an officer of the
Salvation Army, he was lifted shoulder high and carried through the town, while a great procession followed. Two brass bands accompanied the march.

"Well," smiled the Gipsy, overcoming his sadness.
"The band doesn't seem to be playing a retreat." The
musicians were really playing a song to herald a far
greater work than he had ever imagined.

9

The Hero of Hanley

Do not foreclose your religious life by saying "attained" when you have not begun.

Gipsy Smith had a great deal of musical accompaniment in the days following his departure from the Salvation Army! During the ten days of meetings held under the auspices of the Testimonial Committee, Gipsy was carried shoulder-high from place to place, the brass band following. In his own words, he rode "on the crest of a wave." This was more than mere crowd hysteria. When he had come to Hanley as a young Salvationist, Gipsy had only a score of supporters in the town. He had been instrumental in building up the local corps into a large body of live-wire evangelists with whom Gipsy had complete spiritual rapport. He discouraged any dissention within the corps, telling his friends that although he was sorry to be leaving the Army, he felt sure it was in the Lord's will. But the emotional fervor in Hanley could degenerate into a kind of hero worship and, as the Gipsy said on more than one occasion, the Lord can use only those who stay the course. So he went into retreat at Cambridge. Like Jesus Himself, Gipsy drew aside from the crowd in order to pray and to enclose his mind with the will of God.

The good people of Hanley made him promise to return and hold meetings every Sunday and the Imperial Circus was secured for the purpose. The building held four thousand people and it seems that almost every seat was taken for the three meetings held on that first Sunday in 1882, when Gipsy came back from Cambridge. It was obvious to the Testimonial Committee, as to the evangelist, that the meetings should continue, not in any spirit of opposition to the Salvation Army but because so many people were coming to hear the gospel preached. By this time the news of Gipsy Smith's sudden departure from the Salvation Army had spread throughout the country and he was receiving very many invitations to conduct campaigns.

"We need you here, Gipsy," his friends on the Testimonial Committee said. "And God wants you here."

Gipsy left Hanley for another week to rest and to prayerfully consider his future plans. While he was away the people of Hanley worked quickly to demonstrate their determination to keep Gipsy in "the town next to the bottomless pit." The Imperial Circus was secured for three months and a new Testimonial Committee elected, to ensure representation of the Free Churches and the townspeople. Gipsy Smith agreed to stay for a month—a month that proved to be four years long. For nearly two years, the building was crowded every night and for the three services on Sunday. The congregations were the largest outside London. Indeed, in later years, as he traveled the world, Gipsy Smith was to meet many people who came to Christ during the Hanley meetings.

"When I first came to Hanley," he mused, "people used to throw coins at the open-air meetings, thinking we were unemployed laborers. Now I see that the leaders and ministers of very many Free Churches are out in the open air too. There's plenty of work for all of us to do—we are laborers well employed about our Master's business."

Even the minister of St. John's Anglican Parish Church, with his surpliced choir, began to conduct open-air meetings in the market place, afterward marching to the old church, singing "Onward, Christian Soldiers." Gipsy regarded the action of the pastor as the greatest compliment he received at Hanley.

The Sunday night meeting was preceded by an hour's prayer, beginning at 5:30 P.M. The purpose of this was to pray for people without Christ, that they might come into the meeting and be converted—a custom characteristic of the evangelical churches of that period, though it is little practiced now. The prayer meeting was conducted in a large room formerly used, in the days of the circus performances, as a dressing room. It was situated over the stables. One evening, in the October of 1882, as three hundred people were singing praises to God, the floor collapsed, and the congregation fell some ten or eleven feet into the room below. All was pandemonium; arms and legs were broken and more than seventy people injured, but not a life was lost. The crash, heard in the auditorium, inevitably caused some alarm, but the Gipsy, bruised and badly shaken, rushed to the platform to echo those words of Paul, "Do not be alarmed. We are all here and all right!"

The night's excitement had not ended with the accident, however, for the Gipsy had asked the caretaker to turn on full the lights in the auditorium. In his haste, the caretaker turned them all *out*. However, Mr. Brown, the miners' agent, began to sing "Jesus, Lover of My Soul" in the darkness, and the people joined in.

The Gipsy was carried home again after the meeting but this time in exhaustion rather than in triumph. The people hurt in the accident did not miss the blessing of the meetings as they recovered at home, for Gipsy and his friends ensured that they were visited and prayed for. There may have been some structural fault in the building; it was certainly a miracle that all were spared. But the Hanley revival was like that—obstacles were swept aside and people made aware that God was bringing great blessing to the town. Remember that Gipsy Smith was still a young man—in his early twenties, and without the advantages of a good education. It would have been so easy for him to succumb to that ever-present temptation of spiritual pride, of thinking that he could do what ministers could not. But behind the work of this remarkable young man was the sustained prayer of many ministers. Although he saw Cornelius but little, Gipsy had many fathers in Christ at Hanley.

In March 1883, Gipsy and his sister, Tilly, went to Hull to conduct a two-week campaign at Hengler's Circus, a building that had room for some four thousand people. As he arrived at Hull railway station, Gipsy was surprised to see a vast crowd, perhaps as many as twenty thousand people. Many remembered him from the Ice House days; others had read of the

great work being done at Hanley and wanted to share
these good things.

The fortnight passed by but the crowds did not. It
was obvious that the meetings had to be continued.
Gipsy's solution was a sound one—he suggested that
his sister and her fiancé, Mr. Evens, should take
charge of the campaign. They were about to be married, and Mr. Evens already had proved himself an
effective evangelist. Under the supervision of Tilly and
her husband, the Hull campaign was to be wonder-
fully blessed. After some two years at Hull, Mr. Evens
took up the work of a general evangelist and was
succeeded by the then little-known Reverend G. Campbell Morgan. Gipsy knew Campbell Morgan in those
early days and anticipated a great ministry for him.
Maybe this sense of God's possibilities was the secret
of Gipsy Smith's ministry; throughout his life he found
time to encourage young preachers and ministers.

"Let the world see that you mean what you preach,"
he would say, "and God will give you a great ministry."

Although Gipsy did not coin the phrase, I am sure
that he would have agreed with the sentiment that
"opportunity goes around disguised as hard work." It
was hard work at Hanley. In addition to his various
preaching duties, open-air meetings, counseling, and
so forth, Gipsy tried to pursue his studies. Like Dr.
Billy Graham in our own time, he read widely.

"I read for two things," he explained. "For ideas
and a better grasp of the English language. As I
toiled through these pages—for my reading was still
toilsome—I lived in a new world. What an ignorant
child I felt myself to be! I felt confident, too, that
some day the people would find out how little I knew

and get tired of coming to hear me. . . . My soul was possessed with a deep thirst for knowledge, and I greedily drank my fill during the few hours I could find for reading."

In addition to works of English literature and poetry, Gipsy studied the lives of great Methodists, including John Wesley, and read Bible commentaries as well as works by his Christian contemporaries. The books of Charles Finney, Theodore Parker, and Dr. A. McLaren were among those which helped him in his understanding of doctrine and preaching.

Yet, despite the great work given into his hand, Gipsy Smith was not regarded as an ordained minister. This was realized during the autumn sessions of the Congregational Union of England and Wales, held at Hanley in October, 1885. The Free Church ministers prepared the address of welcome and Gipsy was not invited to join in. However, one of the ministers, the Reverend Kilpin Higgs, recognized the folly of leaving out the man who represented the largest congregation in Hanley and explained the situation to the Congregational leaders. Thus, after the Free Church deputation had addressed the Congregational Union, Dr. Thomas, the chairman, invited Gipsy Smith to address the assembly from the platform. This unexpected invitation virtually stunned the Gipsy; he certainly could not recall how he got from his seat onto the platform—but there he was, happy but confused. His words were brief, but well chosen:

"Brothers, I did feel hurt that you did not invite me to accompany you on this occasion. I know that I have not been ordained but I am your brother. I have not had the hand of priest or bishop laid upon my head but I have had the hands of your Lord placed upon me, and I have received His commission to preach the everlasting gospel. If you have been to the cross, I am your brother. If you won't recognize me, I will make you know I belong to you. I am one of your relations."

The delegates applauded loudly, the Gipsy continued: "You see what you have done. If you brethren had invited me to come with you I should have quietly appeared like one of yourselves. But since you ignored me you have made me the hero of the day."

This incident worked for good as well, for Gipsy Smith was inundated by invitations to conduct evangelistic campaigns, and many of these came from Congregational ministers. In December, Gipsy went to Forest Hill, in southeast London, where he conducted meetings at St. James Bible Christian Church, in association with the minister, the Reverend Dr. Keen.

A Christian magazine described it as "a tidal wave of salvation at Forest Hill." Hundreds of people had to be turned away; every inch of standing room in the church was occupied. During the course of these meetings the Gipsy finally recognized that God was calling him to a world-wide ministry, for which Hanley had been preparation. It was an awesome prospect but the young evangelist saw its inevitability. However, he promised he would continue to make his home in Hanley and give his spare time to the mission. So, thanking God for all the blessings that they had enjoyed, the testimonial committee accepted Gipsy Smith's resignation.

Remember, it was General Booth who was responsible for sending him there; all things work together for good to those who trust God. Gipsy Smith named his younger son Hanley, in honor of that town "next to the bottomless pit."

"To the end of my life the name of that town will always arouse joy in my heart," said Gipsy Smith, "and an amazing revelation of what God hath wrought."

10

Faith That Goes Forth

*It is not association with Jesus that saves; it is not
speculation about Him that saves; it is not looking,
nor longing, but contact that saves.*

Few people understand the personal trials that assail
the evangelist and perhaps that is why so many evangelists are criticized. We forget that they are as human
and as frail as the rest of us. Gipsy Smith had his
problems, too. During the years 1886 to 1889 he conducted campaigns throughout England and the success of these missions confirmed his decision to be
an evangelist to the world. But for nine months during
1886 he was unable to preach or sing because of a
throat ailment. A specialist told the Gipsy that his
vocal chords had been unduly strained and that rest
was essential. Coming at the beginning of his itinerant
ministry the ailment placed a considerable burden upon
the Gipsy and his family. Indeed, the savings soon
disappeared and only a few pounds were left when the
evangelist was able to work again. But his friends continued to help him and the Vicar of Brigstock—a
specialist in voice production and control—invited

the Gipsy to stay with him for a fortnight. During
that time the vicar helped the evangelist to understand
the way in which his God-given voice was to be cared
for. It was timely assistance, the kind of sound, practical help which gives any evangelist new heart for his
task. But for the good vicar Gipsy Smith might never
have continued his work which was so soon to take
him to America. In a very real sense the enforced rest
was a disguised blessing, for the visit to America was
both a great opportunity and a difficult task.

Like so many turning points in the life of the
Christian, the American trip started with a casual con-
versation. This was in the Middle East, between Mr.
B. F. Byrom, a cotton spinner of Oldham, and three
ministers. Two of the ministers were from the United
States of America, where they officiated at Congregational churches. The other minister was Dr. R. S.
Macphail, a well-known Presbyterian minister from
Liverpool. They were enjoying a tour of Israel and
Egypt and, inevitably, the conversation turned to spiritual affairs. Mr. Byrom told the Americans about the
young gypsy evangelist who had done so much for the
cause of Christ. The conversation fired the imagination
of the American ministers who pressed Mr. Byrom to
contact Gipsy Smith on their behalf, to inquire if a
campaign in America might be possible. Mr. Byrom
agreed to undertake this errand and did so promptly!
He wrote to the Gipsy as soon as he returned to
England and later had a conversation to point out
the opportunities in a trans-Atlantic campaign.

Gipsy Smith said that he "shrank from such an un-
dertaking." He argued that there was plenty of work
for him to do in Britain.

"So there is," Mr. Byrom said. "But a journey to America would help your education so that you would be all the more able to bring blessing to our own land. In any case, I am certain that God wants you to go."

The Gipsy hesitated but Mr. Byrom saw that only a slight push was necessary to clinch his argument.

"I know that evangelists live by faith," he smiled. "So I will personally guarantee you against any loss in a trip to America."

During the autumn of 1888, when the Gipsy finally agreed to cross the Atlantic, the arrangements were made. But at the very last minute great obstacles arose. One of the American ministers died and the other found himself unable to go ahead with his arrangements. It would have been easy for the Gipsy to have shrugged his shoulders and to cancel the voyage but, by this time, he was determined to go.

He asked various prominent church leaders to write letters of introduction and collected an impressive bundle of recommendations. The Hanley Committee expressed their gratitude for the work that the Gipsy had performed during his seven years' association with the town. "You came as a stranger but soon worked your way into the hearts of the people and hundreds of the worst characters in the town were converted to God. . . . The work has spread, the churches have been quickened, and at the present time in most of the towns and villages of the district successful evangelistic work is carried on." Yes, as the Gipsy said, when the evangelist moves on, the question to be asked is not only, "Do the conversions last?" but "Does the *converting* last?" The evangelist worthy

of the name will always recapture for the local church
the vision of the field ripe unto harvest.

Gipsy Smith boarded the *Umbria* at Liverpool on
January 19, 1889. An uncle (on his mother's side of
the family) traveled a hundred miles in his wagon to
say goodbye to the evangelist. The Gipsy's own description of the farewell is one on which no modern
writer could improve:

"I took him, attired in his gipsy costume, on board
the vessel, and all eyes were upon him. When the
simple man felt the movement of the vessel and saw
the water his eyes filled with tears and, turning to my
wife, he said, 'Annie, my dear, I shall never see him
again.' He had never been on a ship before—he
may, indeed, never have seen one—and he feared that
it could not live in the great mighty ocean. The thought
in his mind was not that he might die before I came
back but that I should probably be drowned. He
asked me, too, if I thought I should have enough to
eat on the way and I managed to assure him on that
point. Presently I took farewell of him—the tears
rolling down his cheeks—my wife, my sister and her
husband, Mr. Byrom and several other friends. I felt
as we slowly sailed away that I was venturing out on
a great unknown, but though my confidence in myself
was poor and weak enough, I was very sure of God."

The Gipsy confessed himself to be a poor
sailor (though that did not discourage him from
visiting America often in subsequent years), and his
first sight of America was on a dismal, wet Sunday
morning, when he came ashore at New York. Mr.
Byrom had advised his friend to find a good hotel and
the Gipsy booked in at the Astor House. It was a

good hotel but it seemed a strange country. On the
following morning he went to the New York Episcopal
Ministers' Meeting and presented a letter of introduction to the president, Dr. Strowbridge. The ministers
gave the visitor a warm welcome although his reputation was little known to them. On Wednesday, Gipsy
Smith went to see Dr. James Buckley, the editor of
The Christian Advocate: however, Dr. Buckley was out
of town, so the evangelist presented his credentials to
Dr. Clark, Dr. Buckley's associate. Although Dr. Clark
was reputed to be out of sympathy with the run-of-the-
mill professional evangelist (and we have to remember
that some rascals had so described themselves in the
latter nineteenth century), he gave Gipsy a sympa-
thetic hearing.

"Well," he said finally, "Dr. Prince of Brooklyn
asked the other day if I knew of a man who could help
him with some special services. I'll give you a note to
take to him."

Dr. Clark took a personal interest in the Gipsy
thereafter and, in the evangelist's opinion, the favorable
press notices in *The Christian Advocate* proved of
invaluable help. We can only assume that the Gipsy
happily restored the doctor's faith in professional
evangelists.

Dr. Prince was the pastor of the Nostrand Avenue
Methodist Episcopal Church, the second largest church
in Brooklyn, itself a sprawling suburb of New York.
A brilliant scholar and preacher, Dr. Prince was also
a very busy man and Gipsy Smith had some difficulty
in gaining admission to his study. However, after
some searching questions from Mrs. Prince, the Gipsy
secured entry and handed over the note from Dr. Clark.

The pastor put on his gold pince-nez and studied the note carefully.

"Well, brother," he said. "I guess I don't want you."

The Gipsy replied calmly, "Well, doctor, I guess that you do."

The reply eased the tension and Dr. Prince smiled.

"I am no adventurer," the evangelist continued. "Perhaps you would like to examine my letters of introduction."

A fair-minded man, Dr. Prince examined the letters and agreed to talk to the official brethren, the deacons, after that evening's service. That night's service, attended by almost three hundred people, was earnest and impressive (as the Gipsy described it). He was told this was the third week of nightly prayer meetings and that a great spirit of supplication had taken possession of the church so that no one felt that the meetings could be discontinued.

Toward the end of the meeting Dr. Prince entered and, seeing the Gipsy in the congregation, introduced him.

"Friends, we have a real live gypsy in the meeting tonight . . . but he is a converted gypsy, and we will ask him to speak to us."

This was an unexpected opportunity for the evangelist and he kept his comments brief. He quietly slipped away while the benediction was being said so that any discussion by the church members could be continued freely. At breakfast the following morning the waiter informed him that Dr. Prince and two gentlemen wanted to speak with him.

They told the Gipsy that they were sure that he had been sent across the ocean to help them and that he should move into the parsonage immediately. This was on Thursday morning and the Americans wanted the Gipsy to begin work on the following Sunday! An announcement about the Gipsy's visit was put into the newspapers and a great spirit of expectancy pervaded the church. The campaign, which lasted three weeks, was a great success. The Nostrand Avenue Church, which seated fifteen hundred people, was crowded at every service, and between four and five hundred people professed to have found the Lord. It was, in Gipsy's view, the fruit of all the prayer meetings being conducted by his friends in England.

"Come to America?" he said. "I would never have stepped foot on the ship had I not known that my work was being supported in prayer."

Just before the beginning of the Brooklyn campaign Gipsy had the pleasure of meeting Ira D. Sankey who, years before, had spoken at a campaign at Bow, in east London. The Gipsy asked Sankey if he recalled a visit to a gypsy encampment in Epping Forest. Sankey said that he did.

"Do you remember that some little gypsy boys stood by the wheel of the carriage in which you were driving and that, leaning over, you put your hand on the head of one of them and said, 'The Lord make a preacher of you, my boy'?"

"Yes, I remember that."

"Well," the Gipsy beamed. "I am that boy."

Sankey was the man who helped Gipsy to maintain high standards of attire for the pulpit. For some unaccountable reason, the evangelist wore no tie although his frock-coat was well-cut and his white shirt and front were brilliant white.

"I guess you'd be wise to wear a white tie, brother Smith," said Sankey. "Otherwise, instead of listening to you some people might just think about your not wearing a tie."

Sankey wanted Gipsy's first impressions upon the people to be as favorable as possible; even a white tie might help, he argued.

Gipsy did not change his preaching style at all for American audiences—he was, as usual, himself. His sermons were simple and his singing appealed to the emotions, as good singing always must. After that memorable Brooklyn campaign the letters of introduction were no longer necessary. Invitations came from many churches and pastors, an impressive vindication of Mr. Byrom's encouragement and assistance.

He was on the way to becoming "the evangelist whom America loved."

11

The Converting Furnace

*Repentance is such a beautiful thing, that Jesus says
when a man or woman does it, there is joy in heaven.*

They were, of course, days when preachers worked
for a decision and not a debate. Such preaching is
largely out of fashion now. I am sure the Gipsy would
sum up our milk and water preaching in some telling
phrase: "When I was out selling my clothespins, I did
my best to make people decide to buy what I had to
offer—I knew that they would be satisfied. Surely, as
a preacher, I have to be at least as enthusiastic as that.
My friends, if the world presented its wares as poorly
as we so often present the gospel, why London would
be full of bankrupts!"

Whatever means of communication we use to express
the gospel, in the final analysis it is simply a matter of
person speaking to person; or rather, God speaking
through one person to another.

During his many visits to America, Gipsy Smith encouraged (and was encouraged by) pastors who
preached as if the present really was the day of salvation. For example, he visited—for the first time in

his life—a congregation of black people during his sojourn in Philadelphia.

"It was a communion service," he wrote, "and about eight hundred of my ebony brethren were present. As far as I could observe I was the only other-colored person in the audience. The opening prayer of the dear old pastor contained many passages characteristic, I believe, of his class: 'O, Lord, thou knowest that this be a well-dressed congregation. Help them to remember that when the offerings to the Lord's work are made. O, Lord, bless the official brethren. Sometimes at their official meetings, they fall out and quarrel. And, Lord, before they take these emblems this afternoon, they need re-converting. Come down and do it, Lord!' At this stage a well-built brother (not one of the official brethren) cried out in a loud and zealous voice: 'Amen, amen, press hard on that point, brother, press hard there!' The pastor continued: 'Lord, go up into the choir and convert the organist!' The organist, who was sitting just behind me, sniffed and said, 'Umph!' It was whispered into my ears that he was the pastor's son-in-law. No one took offense at these very direct petitions, not even the official brethren or the choir or the organist. They all responded 'Amen!' They loved and trusted their old pastor and did not think less of him for the faithfulness of his dealings with them."

The Gipsy enjoyed the fellowship of *all* Christians, not just white ones for, as he argued, "there is not one heaven for the whites, and another for the blacks." On one occasion, a Negro asked the Gipsy what color they would be in heaven.

"I'm not too sure about that," beamed the evangelist, "but I can tell you that we will all be like *Him*."

He had that rare gift of being acceptable to everyone he met. Even when he had achieved fame throughout America a black pastor felt confident enough to
give the Gipsy some good advice.

"Don't tell the people what they want, brother," he
said, "but give them what they *need*."

During his visits to America the Gipsy encountered
many old friends, including some from the great days
of Hanley. He found no greater delight, however, than
in visiting gypsies. The local papers found such events
good copy—indeed, Gipsy Smith's meetings always
had pages of local press coverage, often with his sermon and a description of the meeting included in full.
It must have been a memorable experience for the
young reporter who went with the Gipsy to an
encampment at the Cumminsville Colony in Cincin-
nati. An extract of the report reads like this:

A ROMANY RYE
GIPSY SMITH, THE EVANGELIST IN THE CITY
A ROMANTIC SCENE AT THE CUMMINSVILLE COLONY

There was a rare and decidedly romantic scene
enacted at the gipsy encampment at Cumminsville
yesterday afternoon. Shortly before five o'clock, a
dashing team of bays, with bang-tails, landed upon
the street leading into the centre of the Romany village, with much life. They drew behind them a handsome landau occupied by four gentlemen, and as they
came to a halt in front of the several tents of this
nomadic race there was a shout in the weird language of the gipsies. Instantly, there was a warm
note of recognition from several men with the brown-
hued countenance peculiar to that race standing
nearby, and a number of female heads, bedecked

with gay colours, a weakness of the Romany woman, appeared from the folds of the canvas home.

A neatly-dressed gentleman, with dark complexion and raven-black hair, leaped from the carriage, hat in hand, and for a few minutes the air was full of the nattiest kind of conversation in that strange tongue which men have for years tried to collect, as he shook hands most enthusiastically with those about him.

The new arrival was Gipsy Smith, the famous British evangelist, who twelve years ago gave up the wandering life of his family and turned his attention to preaching the Gospel in his native land, and is now conducting a revival at the Trinity Methodist Episcopal Church.

There was a striking contrast between this civilised Romany Rye and the untamed ones that soon gathered around him. He was attired in a three-button cutaway black coat, and black and grey striped pantaloons, and a white tie peeped out from under a turned-down collar. Surrounding him was a motley gathering of men, women and children. All gazed upon him with great curiosity, but he soon relieved them, and each eagerly tried to talk with him. The young men wore rather shabby attire, with the never-absent coloured handkerchief around their necks. They had but little to say, but one middle-aged, stoutly-built man—as fine a type of the gipsy as mortal man ever looked upon—was unusually friendly.

"I belong to the Smiths," said the evangelist.

"What, from England?"

"Yes, my father was Cornelius Smith!" The Gipsy rattled off a list of the James Smiths that completely threw in the shade the long line of the same noted family in this country.

"Well, well!" cried the big fellow. "I am a Lovell, and my mother was related to the Smiths. Here is my wife." He pointed to a matronly-looking female, enveloped in a faded calico dress, with a white cloth about her head. She took great interest in the stranger, and was soon questioning him about various members of her family.

"We have been in this country twenty-three years but we hear continually from the old 'uns. Times among us over there weren't very good. My poor mother stood it nearly three years in this country when she died," said he of the Lovells.

Peeping into the tent, the evangelist espied a dark-hued woman sitting tailor-fashion upon the ground. She was a perfect specimen of the gipsy fortune-teller of romance. Her ears were ornamented with lengthy pendants of gold, to all appearance; long braids of rich black hair hung over her shoulders. Her head was covered with a wide hat with a brilliant red lining, and in her lap was a young baby with a complexion the richness of which was in striking contrast to the dark olive hue of the mother. Laughing loudly, Smith said in Romany tongue, "What a thorough Gentile baby!" The mother smiled and a sturdy man who stood nearby did not relish the utterance a bit. He was the father and was marked in not having the least resemblance to the race. Smith explained that it was the title always given a child born of the gipsy wife of a husband who was not a Romany.

Lovell and his wife were the only ones in the colony who had ever been abroad, and gradually the talk was confined to them. The others, retiring, gradually dropped out of sight and disappeared either into the shambly tents or walked away to Cumminsville. The little children—and there were two score of them—several of whom were perfect beauties with their dark features and curly hair, returned to their play, and soon had forgotten the distinguished caller.

"Where are all your horses?" was asked of Lovell.

"Oh, the camp is lighter this week than it has been for a long time. Most of our folks are out on the road, and many of our boys and girls will not be back for an hour," was the reply.

"Won't you come down and take a bite with us?" was asked of the evangelist.

"Oh, yes!"

"Make it Sunday?"

"I would like to, but I have three meetings that day."

"All right. We will try to get some of the boys to come down and hear you."

"Say, Lovell, did you ever hear people say we dyed our faces?" continued the evangelist.

"Oh, yes."

"What foolish talk! I can account for the dark complexion. It is due to the long-continued contact with the sun and elements. The poor gypsy is a much-maligned individual."

The newspaper report adds that the Gipsy was highly delighted with the visit and that he said, "Such meetings gave me new zeal in my work." In addition, such genuine interest in the welfare of gypsies was an effective form of evangelistic outreach. Not that churches were always overjoyed to behold a group of gypsies coming into the meeting.

Before the first tour of America came to its conclusion, Gipsy Smith visited Germantown, where Tom Paine wrote *The Age of Reason*. At the time, the house in which Tom Paine had lived was used as a college for young ladies.

Indeed, as the Gipsy wrote, "the room which the infidel writer had used for study was, every morning, used for prayer and Bible reading."

When he returned to Britain, the evangelist used his American experiences as a yardstick for home congregations. "When the church service is over in England everyone rushes for the door, but in America, they rush for one another!"

He emphasized the devotion to prayer found in American churches and the devotion to church buildings characteristic of American Christians.

"There are no shabby strips of coconut-matting in the aisles of American churches," he said. "The schoolrooms, church parlors and vestries are all in keeping with this great respect for the church."

But he was greatly encouraged by the continuing sense of revival and blessing in Britain. He was glad to be back at Hanley, and Hanley was glad to have him, though the good people of the town had by this time accepted that Gipsy's ministry was bound to be world-wide. He spent about a year in England before going back to the United States of America—a year in which he was kept very busy.

The outstanding part of that year's ministry was the ten day campaign at Manchester where the Gipsy worked with Reverend S. F. "Sam" Collier. (Gipsy left Hanley soon after returning to England and worked with S. F. Collier for about a year in all.) Sam Collier was one of the most remarkable evangelists of the century. He pioneered the Central Hall Movement in nineteenth century Methodism. In an attempt to reach the people outside the church, Methodists decided to open a large number of central halls at the heart of British towns and cities. Even today many central halls are still being used. Thus, by helping Sam Collier at Manchester, Gipsy himself was pioneering new methods of evangelism.

The central hall in Manchester was used for this special campaign which had four meetings a day—a meeting for businessmen, an afternoon Bible-reading conducted by F. B. Meyer, the Reverend G. Campbell Morgan or another minister; an eight o'clock service and a midnight service conducted by Reverend S. F. Collier. The midnight services shook Manchester! At ten o'clock every night, 250 campaign workers accompanied by two brass bands proceeded from the central hall to visit bars, music halls, theatres, and other gathering places where they announced the midnight meeting. Congregations numbered from 300 to 600 people, and included down-and-outs, drunks and ne'er-do-wells of almost every kind. A pioneer of audio-visuals, the Reverend S. F. Collier used to get attention with a lantern lecture and in Gipsy's words, "got in the gospel where he could." It was a tough job but amazingly effective. Those down-and-outs were often brought to the essential confession of their own helplessness and then offered restoration through the power of Christ. During the mission some 600 people passed through the inquiry room.

Going to America on the second occasion, in August, 1891, Gipsy Smith could look forward to a warm welcome, a great contrast to that first voyage into the unknown. He sailed on the *Etruria* from Liverpool.

His first campaign was at Old Jane Street Methodist

Episcopal Church, in New York. The Reverend
Stephen Merritt, pastor of the church, was an amazing
evangelist himself. While still a layman, he preached
with such results that the Bishop of the Diocese gave
him charge of the Old Jane Street Church.

The campaign was held in September, a very hot
month in New York.

"It's certainly warm, brother," the Gipsy smiled. "Do
you think that the people will want to come inside?"

"They call my church a tremendous converting
furnace," the minister replied. "They'll come—in
crowds."

And they did. Hundreds accepted Christ in that "tremendous converting furnace." The Gipsy especially remembered the young couple who came to the church
to be married and who decided to stay for the evangelistic service. Within two hours of their marriage ceremony they had come forward to accept Jesus Christ. As
the Gipsy said, "they commenced their new life under
the very best of bonds."

12

The Fruit at the Top of the Tree

*All the preachers in the universe, all the professors
who ever walked the corridors of the seminaries, all
rolled into one mighty brain could not have invented
this doctrine. Jesus said it. He turned away from the
affairs of state eternal, from adoration of angels to
whisper into your ear and mine, "You must be born
again."*

During the nineteenth century, self-supporting com-
munities were very popular in America—new citizens
were determined to make a new life in the New World.
Gipsy Smith visited a rather unusual community, Ocean
Grove, during his tour of 1891. Ocean Grove was
founded by a small group of Methodist preachers who
knew it first as an ideal camping ground. They decided to establish a permanent camping site for use
by all Christians. It was a very successful project and,
at the time of Gipsy's visit, Ocean Grove was already a
city of several thousand people, managed by a Methodist association. The population grew to seventy or
eighty thousand during the camping season, when people came from all parts of America to hear the great
speakers booked for the convention. Gipsy Smith liked
Ocean Grove, which he described as a favorite holiday
resort for American pastors (a modest enough observation, when one recalls that as many as 250 ministers

could be seen on the platform during the convention meetings). Trains were not permitted to stop at Ocean Grove on Sundays, and no milk or mail could be delivered on that day. True to the original Methodist tradition, no bars were permitted. But, before we dismiss the good people of Ocean Grove as narrow-minded, it is as well to emphasize that the town was an orderly and happy place. During his stay Gipsy Smith did not see a single policeman, and only one uniformed official was required to keep the large crowds in order.

The auditorium seated some ten thousand people, and three meetings were held every day during the convention season. Two meetings for young people were held daily in the Ocean Grove Temple but, as the Gipsy observed, the phrase *young people* seemed to apply to anyone below the age of ninety. There is no doubt that Ocean Grove was a powerhouse for evangelism; ministers told the Gipsy that, but for these meetings, many churches in America would have closed long before. On this occasion the Gipsy was as much observer as participant. It was certainly a mark of his growing fame in America that he was asked to attend, for the organizers of the convention were men with feet firmly on the ground, eager to take a new zeal for evangelism back to local churches. So, for ten days, the Gipsy made friends among Christians of virtually every Christian denomination, and he certainly learned a few ideas about public speaking. He was very impressed by the personal testimonies, then so much a feature of church life.

"The Americans," Gipsy observed, "are more ready than are we British to give a reason for the hope that is in them." In a very real sense Gipsy took that theme across the world with him. One young preacher, years later, told the evangelist that he found it difficult to write sermons.

"Just tell them what Jesus means to you," the Gipsy advised him. "Tell them why you're a Christian—and you'll find enough reasons to make a whole series of sermons."

Ocean Grove also shaped the plan of the tour. After giving two addresses at the young people's meetings, the Gipsy received many requests to visit local churches; more, indeed, than he could manage on that trip. Already he must have been thinking of a possible third tour.

It would be quite impossible to catalogue all the events of the 1891 tour. One can simply say that the USA took Gipsy Smith into her generous heart. He returned to the Nostrand Avenue Methodist Church in New York, where he had first preached to Americans. To his delight he discovered that many who had been converted during his first visit to the church were now active members, doing their best to build up the congregation.

One evening, he had hardly entered the pulpit when he saw a gypsy and a lady, obviously the gypsy's wife, in the congregation. At the end of the service Gipsy Smith met the couple and learned that they had pitched their tent just outside Brooklyn. They were not poor gypsies, but given to the characteristic roaming life of the Romany. Invited to visit the camp, Gipsy Smith gladly accepted, and so did six ladies of the church. The evangelist, to the end of his days, worked to break down the barrier of misunderstanding between the Romanies and the "gentiles," so he was delighted to take the ladies with him. They had a wonderful time. There were not sufficient cups to go around so some members of the party drank their tea from saucers. The Gipsy always enjoyed visiting people of his race. "I never know when I might meet one of my distant relations," he used to say.

The most successful campaign in New York was that at the Calvary Methodist Episcopal Church in Harlem. The pastor, Dr. James Roscoe Day, was a remarkable preacher, who usually addressed crowded congregations. So the preparation for the campaign had been well done. This is an important point. The Gipsy emphasized, time and time again, that his visits could only be used by God when the church had already trimmed its lamps through prayer and sacrifice.

"Some people expect you to freeze in the vestry and blaze in the pulpit," he said. "Pray for great things, work for great things, expect great things."

The campaign at Calvary Methodist Episcopal Church lasted for a month—a month that went all too quickly. Very many people were converted, children and old men alike, even entire families. The Gipsy would have extended the campaign, but other engagements pressed upon him. At the end of the campaign, an "illuminated address" was presented to the evangelist. "We believe Gipsy Smith to be an evangelist particularly called by God to His work, the possessor of rare gifts as an expounder of the truth and a winner of men. We believe our membership has been greatly quickened spiritually, and through our brother's instrumentality many souls have been added to the church." Dr. Day and the twenty-four members of the church's official board signed the statement, and also presented the Gipsy with handsome remuneration for his services. The ladies of the church sent a gift of £20 to his wife—"the wife who had so generously allowed me to cross the Atlantic to help and bless them."

But the campaign was not without its critics. One Monday morning the Gipsy accompanied Dr. Day to the regular meeting of the New York Methodist ministers. Dr. Day told his colleagues about the work at the Calvary Methodist Episcopal Church, which he described as "a revival on old-fashioned Methodist lines." A well-respected minister present did not share this enthusiasm.

"I don't believe in evangelists," he stated. "I've been in the ministry for many years and I have never had an evangelist in my church and I never shall. When the wind blows, the dust blows, and when the wind settles, the dust settles. I believe in hand-picked fruit, in conversions which result from the ordinary work of the ministry. But I am glad to see Gipsy Smith present this morning and I shall be glad to hear him."

The ministers called for Gipsy Smith to reply, but he was reluctant to become involved in any controversy. After all, as he explained, he was a stranger in a strange land and God's work was always vindicated by its results, not what men said about it.

But the ministers insisted that the evangelist reply. It must have been a memorable morning for all of them, for the Gipsy stated the purpose of evangelism in a way that could be little improved upon today.

"It may be a very smart thing to say that when the wind blows, the dust blows, and when the wind settles, the dust settles, but it is not a Christ-like thing to say of a brother and his work. If God has given to the church evangelists, it is because you need them. What God has called clean, do not you call common. You say that you believe in hand-picked fruit, so do I. It fetches the highest price in the market, but what are you to do when the fruit is too high for you to reach it and you have no ladder? Everybody knows, too, that some of the best fruit is at the top of the tree. Are you going to lose that fruit because you are not tall enough or strong enough to get it? I won't! I will ask the first godly brother that comes along to help me shake that tree and will get the fruit though we bruise it in the getting. I would rather not have said this. I do not believe in defending myself or setting myself against my brethren in the ministry. I have always tried to be the pastor's help, and I never allow myself in public or private to say anything which disparages one of my brethren. It hurts and grieves me when I hear a pastor speaking disdainfully of the work of an evangelist, remembering as I do that God has given to the Church some apostles, some prophets, some evangelists, as well as pastors and teachers."

His words had a powerful effect. Later, Gipsy had a conversation with the minister who had criticized his work and they parted good friends. Gipsy Smith could never bear to leave anyone on bad terms. He spoke his mind, and never pulled his punches—but only because he wanted others to see the truth and, in doing so, come into some greater work for the Lord.

A Roman Catholic priest's conversion was the highlight of the New York campaign at Old Bedford Street. Speaking to the penitents at the communion rail one evening the Gipsy—who had been preaching on "Jesus, the only Cure"—was called upon to counsel a handsome man, who proved to be a Roman Catholic priest. The Gipsy recalled that the Reverend Father O'Connor, a former priest and well known for his work among Catholics, was in the audience and so he sought his assistance. On the following day the young priest and the Gipsy dined with Father O'Connor, and the convert went on to become an evangelist after resigning from his church.

The Gipsy had certainly shaken "the fruit from the top of the tree" during his work in New York. But now it was time to go home. The Gipsy had been away from his family for seven months.

"Seven months?" he said. "It seems more like seven years to me." And, as the ship steamed up the Mersey, he reflected that no city ever looked as grand as Liverpool did that day.

13

The Children

You may make a mark on time that will not be rubbed out in eternity.

Gipsy Smith had three children—Zillah, his daughter, and two sons, Albany and Hanley. We know little of the Gipsy's domestic life during that first hectic decade of his ministry but he was always overjoyed to return home to his family. Like any evangelist's wife, Mrs. Annie Smith had a challenging ministry of her own, for the Gipsy could never have done so much without her care (a fact which he often mentioned). She was a gracious woman, possessing that self-effacing quality sometimes mistaken for timidity. In early middle age she appears—in photographs—as a well-built woman with soft curly hair, a smooth and slightly studious face, and clear, intelligent eyes behind gold-rimmed spectacles. One cannot but feel that Annie Smith (née Pennock) was a personality in her own right. Nevertheless, she tended to let her husband do all the talking, off the platform as well as on it.

With her husband's journeying throughout the country and, indeed, much of the world, Annie Smith had the task of acting as father as well as mother to her three children. It was not easy. The Gipsy, on being asked what was the hardest part of his work, replied "Being away from my family. It's a great privilege to be an evangelist, but don't let anyone tell you that it is an easy task."

The children had their problems, too. Albany, when still quite young, was taunted by his school chums as being "a gypsy kid." Albany punched the offender in the nose but, when the boy's nose began to bleed, took him home to repair the damage. Gipsy Smith obtained the full story from his son and pointed out that he was the son of a gypsy and that was really a great privilege.

"I know that, Father," said Albany. "But no one is going to call me 'a gypsy kid.'"

The children were at the receiving end of prejudice against the gypsy race on a few occasions. Indeed, the evangelist had some experiences which were almost laughable, like that of the little boy who, on encountering Gipsy Smith, looked open-eyed, and somewhat fearful.

"You're not frightened of me, are you?" smiled the evangelist.

"I say, it's not true, is it?" countered the lad.

"What isn't true?"

"That you're one of those gypsies that catch hold of little boys and take away all their clothes!"

"Of course not," smiled the Gipsy. "Who told that fine yarn to you?"

"My nurse," said the child. "And I'm glad that she's wrong."

On another occasion, the evangelist was amused by a little boy's definition of a gypsy—"someone who goes around seeing what he can pick up."

Once, the Gipsy was due to stay at a house for a few

days but the son of the household refused to meet the guest and went to stay with his grandmother.

"Children are often told silly stories about gypsies," the evangelist wrote. "And they create prejudices that poison."

But, true to his calling, he overcame evil with good. He was a superb storyteller and had a natural instinct for talking to children. Some of them seemed to be disappointed that he did not wear the colorful attire of the gypsies and just a few refused to believe that he was a member of that race.

"Are you *really* a gypsy?"

"Yes, really a gypsy."

"Then where's your wagon?"

And there were just a few potential delinquents, like the little girl living at a house in which the Gipsy was staying. He attempted to begin a conversation with her, first by saying what pretty eyes she had, then by referring to her lovely dress. There was no reply to either of these observations but the Gipsy continued trying. Eventually the little girl, with a look of scorn, said: "You didn't even notice I've got new shoes on."

"There's one thing about children," the Gipsy used to say. "You can always tell if they're listening to you or not. Some grown-ups can look wide awake when they've really dropped off to sleep mentally. But children don't let you have any illusions as to whether or not you're reaching them."

Of course, he was very eager to bring his own children to Christ. One evening the Gipsy came home after speaking at a meeting, only to discover that his children were playing at having a meeting of their own. The main purpose of this may well have been to stay up that little longer but the Gipsy decided to join in with the spirit of the proceedings. Albany led the impromptu meeting and, after a couple of hymns, called upon his father to speak: "Now, we shall have Brother Gipsy Smith's experiences!"

The father spoke to his children in earnest and told them of all that God had done for him since those days when he was just a boy in a gypsy tent. "God had done so much for me . . . and He will surely do even greater things for you, if you but surrender your lives to Him." For such a small congregation the Gipsy preached a powerful message. Albany stood up and declared the meeting closed.

Zillah was already proving her abilities as a singer and, as the children often arranged meetings like the one described above, she gained plenty of singing practice. But she insisted on a proper introduction, even if the audience consisted of just the living room furniture.

"Miss Zillah Smith will now favor us with a solo!" Well, the Gipsy learned his craft by preaching to the turnips, so it was not entirely inappropriate that his daughter gained hers by singing to tables and chairs. In later years Zillah was often to sing solos at the Gipsy's meetings.

Albany had at least one occasion to rebuke his father, though rebuke is certainly too strong a word for the experience, which caused the Gipsy considerable amusement. Albany and Hanley attended Tettenhall College in Wolverhampton and were frequent visitors to the Queen Street church, where Dr. Charles Berry was pastor. The Gipsy conducted a ten-day campaign at the church and, on the two Sundays, the sons were allowed to sit in the platform party. During one of the afternoon meetings the Gipsy spoke about his home life and referred to his sons on the platform. Later, Albany—then about fifteen years of age—said to his father: "Look here, if you are going to make me conspicuous like that, I don't want to come to any more of your meetings." But he was so proud of his father that night that, when the sermon was over, young Albany walked up the pulpit steps to kiss his father good-night.

"Well, well," said the Gipsy. "You're making *me* conspicuous now!"

The children shared their father's love for the gypsy race and Zillah dressed as a gypsy girl when invited to recite a poem by Tennyson on a high school exhibition day at Manchester.

She thoroughly enjoyed going to meetings with her father. At one church a steward had a very unfortunate and unfriendly manner, so that people coming into the building sought to avoid him. Zillah noticed him almost at once and asked her father: "Is Jesus like that man, Daddy?"

"No, my dear," he replied. "Why do you ask?"

"Because if He is, I shall run away. But if Jesus is like someone I know, I shall put my arms around His neck and kiss Him."

As he observed in his autobiography, children know what Jesus is about, and they seldom make a mistake.

When she was still only nine years of age, Zillah walked with her father on their way to church. The Gipsy found two little lambs straying on the road and carefully lifted them back into the adjoining field, saying almost to himself, "All we like sheep have gone astray."

"That would be a good text to preach from," said Zillah.

"And how would you preach from that?" her father inquired.

"Well, I think I would begin by saying God was the shepherd and we were the sheep, and that He has a fold and we have got out of it. Then I should try to make it very plain that Jesus comes to find the sheep and bring them back again to the right place, as you did just now."

Gipsy's nephew, young Bramwell Evens, thought the world of his uncle and the greatest punishment that could be inflicted upon him was when his mother—Gipsy's sister, Tilly—told him that she would tell his uncle about it. Mr. Evens was an evangelist too and, on one occasion, Bramwell and his mother were waiting in the vestry of a church in which he was holding a campaign. Bramwell had been naughty, and his mother said that his uncle should be told.

"Can I be saved?" asked the boy.

"Of course," said Tilly. "If you are in earnest."

"Please kneel down and pray for me, then," he implored.

As his mother began to pray, the vestry door opened and a little boy, with whom Bramwell was on poor terms, entered. At once, Bramwell got up and shook his fist at the intruder.

"Go away," he roared. "Can't you see that I'm getting saved?"

Bramwell had merely been attempting a maneuver to prevent his uncle being told of his misdeeds. Uncle was presumably told. The tale must have provoked considerable amusement in later years when Bramwell was himself a Methodist minister and a beloved broadcaster of his "Romany" program.

One can imagine that, at any slip of the tongue or lapse of memory, someone would say, "Bramwell, we'll have to tell your uncle!"

14

The Bull's-Eye

*I believe that it is better to have a fence at the edge
of the precipice than a hospital at the bottom.*

The Gipsy was still only in his early thirties when he
went to Edinburgh, that home of great preachers, to
conduct a fortnight's campaign at the Fountain Bridge
Free Church, in May 1892. The church proved too
small for all who wished to enter, and so a final meeting was held at the large and famous St. George's
Church, where Dr. Alexander Whyte was minister. It
was a memorable occasion. The Gipsy told the story of
his life—"The Gospel and the Gypsy Tent"—and it
spoke, as clearly as any sermon, of the power of God
to transform lives, however low.

Dr. Whyte, who presided at the meeting, paid tribute to the Gipsy's gifts: "I have heard many great
men in that pulpit but I have never felt my heart so
moved as it was tonight by your story. I do not envy
the man who listened to it with dry eyes."

In the many years of fruitful service still ahead and unknown at that time, the Gipsy almost always closed his
campaigns with his life story. At the turn of the century, he was pressed to have the story printed and,
aided by Mr. W. G. Berry, he produced a manuscript in
1901. Mr. W. G. Berry was the editor of "The Sunday

at Home," one of England's most popular Christian weeklies. *Gipsy Smith—His Life and Work,* by himself, was a best-seller, reprinted many times. By 1905, it had already sold fifty-five thousand copies and the manuscript was revised a number of times to incorporate additional material: the Gipsy's work in the First World War, for example, being added to the 1920 edition.

But the Gipsy was far more than a sentimental storyteller. The minister of the Fountain Bridge Free Church, the Reverend George D. Low, M.A., reported the campaign for the *British Weekly* of June 23, 1892, and gave a graphic description of the Gipsy's preaching style:

> Gipsy Smith is a born orator with great dramatic fire, of singular intensity of spirit. His voice is tuneful and flexible, and lends itself readily to the expression of every mood of mind and every form of discourse. He is specially effective when he illustrates and illuminates some point, or some Gospel truth, by an incident simple, tender, pathetic, from his old gipsy life, to which he frequently alludes, as one proud of his origin. His addresses are Scriptural, as might be expected from one who is an unwearied and resolute student of the Bible. In manner, he is simple, unaffected, gentlemanly, and I can speak the more confidently regarding this as he lived under my roof while in Edinburgh, and gained the esteem and affection of every member of my household by his sunny, gracious personality. His singing, which is of great purity and excellence, adds greatly to his power. From first to last, no fewer than 150 professed their faith in Jesus Christ.

It was during his stay in Edinburgh that Gipsy was instrumental in forming the Gipsy Gospel Wagon Mission. Like his father, he was very concerned about the low moral state of many gypsies, few of whom knew anything about the Bible and its message. During that final evening in Edinburgh the evangelist had spoken of his desire to bring Christ to the gypsies, through some kind of parsonage on wheels. As he was about to leave the city on the following morning a lady came to the manse and asked to speak to the Gipsy. She explained that, having heard the Gipsy's call for help on behalf of the Romanies, she wished to pay for a first wagon. During conversation with the Gipsy she mentioned having visited a gypsy camp many years earlier, while visiting the poor in Lancashire. She spoke to a gypsy woman, then very ill and, from the visitor's description, Gipsy Smith recognized the sick woman as having been his aunt (his mother's brother's wife).

Although the Gipsy could take little active part in the work of the Gipsy Gospel Wagon Mission, he enlisted the aid of many of his friends, including Dr. Alexander Whyte, Dr. S. Macphail, Reverend S. F. Collier and Mr. B. F. Byrom. The Gipsy himself donated the proceeds of the lectures he gave on his life and, over the years, this proved the main source of income, although donations were also received. The first evangelist for the mission was Mr. John Wesley Baker and, as the Gipsy well realized the loneliness that often afflicts those traveling alone, he arranged for the missionary to have an assistant. The wagon traveled all over Britain and was especially useful in places where gypsies congregated for fairs and amusement.

But the Gipsy warned his friends to prepare for dis-

couragement. "Evangelistic work among the gypsies is
slow and hard," he said. "My people have quick eyes,
quick ears and ready tongues. But for years—indeed,
for centuries—their hearts have been blinded to the
things of God. There is hardly a race on this globe to
whom religious faith is so utterly foreign. The gypsies
are slow to comprehend the plan of salvation, and even
when they have understood they are slow to use it because, for one thing, their trade is declining. They are
depending more and more on the fortune-telling, and
and they know very well that if they become Christians
that lying practice must cease."

One wonders what the Gipsy would make of the
Christians who consult their newspaper horoscope every
day. The Gipsy's reaction would be: "Why, you're
worse than the gypsies! At least, they don't know any
better!" The Gipsy, in his preaching, was an advocate
for all-out Christianity.

In the August of 1892 he returned to America—
this time taking his wife. He received a hearty welcome
at Ocean Grove where large crowds waited to hear
him. There, too, he preached of the Saviour. Indeed
his preaching was so persuasive that a black woman
preacher in the congregation cried out, "That's hit the
bull's-eye, Brother Smith. Now, hit it again!" During
this tour the Gipsy had several opportunities of helping people to find Christ. It is easier to preach to large
crowds about Christ than to speak to the lonely, puzzled individual. Certainly, it was a mark of the Gipsy's
real commitment to his cause that he took time to speak
to the individual—if the individual really was concerned. The Gipsy encountered many people who pre-
tended to be interested in becoming a Christian but

who really wished no more than to "touch the man for themselves."

One lady approached the Gipsy and said that she had been seeking Christ for ten years. The Gipsy assured her that there was something wrong if a seeking Saviour and a seeking sinner had yet to meet each other after ten years—adding that this could easily be put right. The woman said that she had heard the best evangelists, read the best books, almost memorized sermons from the best preachers.

"Well, now," said the Gipsy quietly, "what you need isn't men or meetings, but an interview with Jesus Himself. You go home and shut yourself away for a while, and simply ask God to come into your life. What you need to do is to go through the crowds, just like the woman who touched the hem of the Lord's garment, and simply touch *Him*."

The next day she met him again and, from the happiness on her face, it was obvious that she had found peace of mind. The Gipsy had hit the bull's-eye again!

"We preachers must make it easy for people to find Christ," he said. "We must avoid erecting man-made barriers, of using long words that the ordinary people cannot understand. I don't underestimate the many trials that face the Christian, but neither do I underestimate the power of the Lord to save *and* to keep."

The Gipsy conducted missions in many parts of America during 1892, including Lynn, near Boston and at Philadelphia, where the campaign had to compete with the party atmosphere of the presidential election. On election night the crowds at the church were larger than ever, thus confounding the faint hearts who had suggested canceling the meeting. Most of the campaigns

were conducted under the auspices of the Methodist
Episcopal Churches but at Yonkers, on the Hudson
River, the Gipsy held a united church campaign. This
was one of the happiest campaigns he ever conducted.
There was a noticeable spirit of freedom and joy in all
the meetings—and how the people were converted!
One night, a lad of ten came into the inquiry room and
returned the following night with his mother. On the
night after that, mother and son returned with the
lad's grandmother.

The evangelist made many friends at Yonkers, including two of the ministers, Dr. Hobart and Dr. Cole.
The ministers presented Gipsy with an illuminated
scroll at the close of the campaign. The inscription
was simple: "To the 'Rev.' Rodney Smith. We love
you with the love of brothers and we are sure we shall
meet when our work and yours is done, and love you
through eternal years in heaven."

Throughout his life Gipsy Smith enjoyed generous
coverage from the American press. Local newspapers
would print not only a full account of all the prelimi-
naries and a resume of the Gipsy's life, but also the
text of his sermon. The Gipsy would chuckle whenever
he saw that the press "went to town" in this way.

"Why, they are becoming evangelists, too," he exclaimed. In America then, as today, there tended to
be more Christians in journalism than in Britain—
simply on the basis that church membership was so
much more part of the good life. Take, for instance,
the article on Gipsy's campaign at Yonkers, printed in
a very self-respecting newspaper, *The Yonkers' Gleaner*:

> Gipsy Smith is a notable evangelist, notable for
> what he is, as a warm hearted, frank, honest, ef-

fective preacher. He knows how to persuade men.
He deals with great truths. His views of truth are
in accord with the best thoughts of those who have
had advantages far greater than his. He is an instance
of what great wisdom can be gotten from the Scriptures by a man who is truly converted. It tells us
again, by example, that in the Scriptures "the man
of God is thoroughly furnished unto every good
work". We honour him as a man sent of God to
gather harvests.

But he is notable for what he will not do. He
did not condemn the ministry nor the churches,
though he spared not the sins that were found in
them. He did not get mad when inquirers were slow
to make themselves known. He did not assume to
decide who were saved and who were not. He did
not put a drop of vitriol on the end of his sentences
concerning the wicked or the unfaithful, as if he
enjoyed the opportunity to say "hell". He did not
spend a whole evening descanting on the sex or
gender of the Holy Spirit, though he holds no un-
certain opinion about it. He did not preach a sermon
on the unpardonable sin (!!) as a flaming sword to
drive people into the inquiry room. He did not for
once make an effort to be funny—he is too much in
earnest. He did not appeal for money, and did not
hurt his cause by telling stories that slurred sacred
things. He came in love, he spoke in earnest. He was
full of sanctified common sense. He won our hearts.
He did us all good. May choice blessings follow his
efforts.

This editorial is an interesting mixture of "journa-
lese" and of church public relations. In listing those
acts *not* done by the Gipsy, one might almost ask if
men who did these things were known. Perhaps so—

every true evangelist has to combat the bad memories left by men who called themselves evangelists but who showed little of the Lord in their personal dealings with churches or converts.

The Gipsy hit the bull's-eye on another occasion. Paying a return visit to the Calvary Methodist Episcopal Church in New York, he noticed a young man who came to many of the services but who failed to give his life to Christ. The Gipsy was determined that the young man would come onto the right side. One day, providentially, he met the young man on Broadway, and asked if he would be at that evening's meeting. The young man hesitated, explaining that he had a previous engagement.

"All right," smiled the Gipsy. "Then will you pray for me?"

"But I haven't prayed for myself for years," the other replied, aghast.

"Never mind," persisted the Gipsy. "Just pray for me."

The young man tried to avoid the favor the Gipsy asked of him. But the evangelist wrote a short prayer onto a piece of paper.

"There you are," he said, "I've written this short prayer—Dear God, bless Gipsy Smith tonight and help him to preach Thy gospel in the power of the Holy Spirit so that sinners may be converted. For Christ's sake. Amen. Now, I just want you to say those words for me tonight, wherever you are." The Gipsy thrust the paper into the young man's hand and did a little silent praying himself.

On the following evening the Gipsy kept a sharp

lookout for the young man and was delighted to see him enter the church, now looking far happier.

"You knew what you were doing," the young man told the evangelist. "As soon as I knelt down to say this prayer, I felt like the meanest man in America. I had neglected God for years. In my distress, I could not pray for you at first . . . but I prayed for forgiveness of myself. He saved me and then I prayed for you."

The young man shook the evangelist's hand and then, like so many others, went off to live out the Christian life in his own small corner.

"We ministers and evangelists must cultivate the greatest skill in throwing out the gospel net," the Gipsy wrote in his autobiography. "In the work of saving men, we need to use all the brains we have and to *think* for God as earnestly and as thoroughly as we think for our business."

15

The Preacher

God has a service for some of you that angels envy—
if they can envy!—something for you to accomplish
that whets the appetite of an angel. Be careful!

It was during the 1890's that the Gipsy evolved the
preaching style that was to mark his ministry in the
years ahead. The fervor of youth became tempered with
the gentleness of maturity—in earlier years, some
could say that he was no more than a boy wonder, that
it was his youth more than his message that attracted
the crowds. The Gipsy matured early in life; he had
little enough time in which to grow up. Today, a few
people can remember his sermon style at the turn of
the century. The sermon themes were basic and ones
that he was to repeat many times.

Take, for example, one of the Gipsy's encounters at
the Calvary Methodist Episcopal Church in New York
in 1893. A well-dressed man asked the Gipsy to pray
for him not once but several times, yet seemed to re-
ceive no relief or blessing. The Gipsy counseled the
man and discovered that he was a backslider. It seemed
that the man had once been a worker in a Sunday
school but had given it up in a temper.

"Ah, there it is," said the Gipsy. "You rejected the

work that God had given you. You must return to it before you will find peace in your heart."

The man hesitated but did as the evangelist suggested. A few days later he returned, happier and restored to the fellowship. "I did as you told me, and all the old joy came back!"

The Gipsy, in his autobiography, stated his belief that the incident shows a great lesson for Christians disappointed in the spiritual life. "When they sing, 'Where is the blessedness I knew, when first I saw the Lord?' I reply that it is where you left it. You have been dropping some of your Christian work. Go back to it and you will find the blessing there. God is the same. It is only you that have changed."

This theme became established in his sermon, "The Lost Christ," heard by thousands—and perhaps millions by radio throughout the world. "If you have lost that blessedness that first you knew, it is because you have left Christ not because He has left you. And He is waiting for you just where you left Him."

This was not sentimental meandering, although the Gipsy was certainly an emotional preacher. In these difficult times we often overlook the teaching of Scripture on being reconciled to one's brother before coming to the altar. The Gipsy could claim that he had seen families reconciled, wrongs forgiven, even people in the church brought together after years of resentment. Two of the strongest words for good in the whole English language are, "I'm sorry," the Gipsy used to say.

Another sermon theme was that of repentance, a subject not often encountered in our own times. It is worth remembering that the majority of people at meetings conducted by Gipsy Smith were church members. These were the very people who came forward to the communion rail when the Gipsy made his appeal. It is easy to imagine the impact of this fiery evangelist in some great church full of people, but the truth of the matter is that, even in relatively small groups, using his basic sermon material, the Gipsy was equally effective.

During his visit to America in 1893, the Gipsy was invited to conduct drawing room meetings (what we would call house meetings today) at Fifth Avenue, New York. About 175 people were present at the first meeting; if anything, the surroundings might well have inhibited the preacher. It is easier to preach among bare boards and sparse furnishings than in the luxury of a wealthy American home. But the Gipsy seemed at ease. "I just remembered that these people were sinners in need of a Saviour," he said.

The meeting lasted a little over an hour and, at the end of it, one of the ladies present confessed, "If that that is true religion, then I know nothing of it." Another lady sought counseling. "All you have to do, my dear, is to follow Jesus," the Gipsy told her. Seven meetings were held and there were some remarkable blessings.

The Gipsy preached for conversions. That, he explained, was his ministry. He knew that he could do little in the way of building up the church through the teaching of doctrine—and, in any case, that was not his job.

At about this time, a Mrs. Davies of Southsea heard him in one of the English campaigns. Her memory gives us a precious description of a meeting during the eighteen-nineties:

"In 1895, I was eighteen years of age. I was very religious and came from a respectable family, my father being a farm bailiff in Folkestone, Kent. I was a member of the Church of England.

"One day, my sister-in-law took me to the Railway Mission where the evangelist Gipsy Smith was speaking. I had never been into such a place before, and it was filled to capacity. The hymns—well! I thought that they could not be hymns because of the way they were sung. I had never heard such singing, it was such a difference to the choir with which I was so familiar.

"I went only once to this Railway Mission but I still remember, even at 92 years of age, the text which the Gipsy preached on. I recall him driving the message home: 'Whosoever calleth on the name of the Lord *shall* be saved.' Saved! I thought, whatever does he mean? Of course we are saved. My Bible was put away so as not to get dirty: it was my most treasured possession. I kept it covered and free from dust, but *never* read it.

"Some time later I heard some young people singing on the seafront and this was just like the singing I had heard at the Railway Mission. Again, I heard the message on sin. Then I remembered Gipsy Smith's words, 'Whosoever shall call upon the name of the Lord *shall* be saved.' That night I knelt at my bedside and gave my heart to the Lord Jesus Christ. The next morning I felt so happy I wanted everybody to hear about Jesus."

Another lady, then also about eighteen years of age, recalls the Gipsy's meetings at the Albert Hall, Nottingham:

"He was a handsome, dark-skinned gypsy of medium

stature, brown eyes, radiant expression of his great love for the Lord Jesus, of a special gentleness, always filled with joy.

"Gipsy Smith preached of his great love for the Lord Jesus Christ, and one could hear a pin drop—such was the great attention of his hearers. I remember playing the piano while he sang. He had a rich tenor voice. We sang duets together, mostly Sankey and Moody hymns. One I particularly remember was, 'We Walk by Faith But Not Alone.' I remember his pleading voice expressing the need to commit oneself to Jesus. He gave many anecdotes referring to flowers in his sermons. His lovely illustrations were almost poetry.

"During his stay at the Edwalton Manor House he was more than thrilled to be taken with my mother in a landau carriage behind a couple of blue roans with bells ringing on their harness. There was no tar on the roads in those days."

Of course, there are things to recall with a smile, also. In one of the services at Dobs Ferry, the Gipsy told the story of Zaccheus and at the words, "Zaccheus, come down," Mr. Fields—host to the evangelist—fell from his camp stool! Fortunately, he was not hurt (except his dignity, perhaps!). Mr. Fields, a good friend to the Gipsy, took him to Albany, the capital of New York State. The president of the legislative assembly warmly greeted the visitor and invited him to open the meeting in prayer.

"Ah," the Gipsy said, "I expect that I will have to wait a long time before a similar invitation is extended to me from Westminster." In fact, Lloyd George, one of Britain's most prominent statesmen, later became one of his best friends.

16

Tomfoolery in Glasgow

There is a faith which saves and there is an intellectual faith which damns!

If the seat of Parliament at Westminster had yet to invite the Gipsy, the good folk of Glasgow were quicker to see the possibilities of evangelism. A number of Free Church ministers formed a committee and invited Gipsy Smith to conduct a campaign in their city. Apart from a brief break for Christmas, the campaign lasted from September, 1893 to January, 1894, seven weeks of which he spent in seven different churches without giving the same sermon twice! It was a remarkable campaign.

At first the natural reserve of the Scottish character (as he called it) produced something of a barrier between the large congregations and the preacher in the pulpit. But no fewer than three thousand people passed through the inquiry room for counseling. The history of many of these conversions was unusual. Many of those subsequently converted first came to hear the Gipsy through curiosity (rather like Zaccheus going to see Jesus). Then they would become interested in the services and would follow the Gipsy from church to church in the city, hearing his preaching which slowly was accepted. "In some cases," the Gipsy reported, "the people who came into the inquiry room had heard me preach during the entire campaign, but it took several weeks to bring them to a place of surrender to God."

At one service the Gipsy did not even preach, because the people began to go into the inquiry room after the singing of the hymn. The Gipsy thought that many of the people had made up their minds to come forward even before coming to church. His comments on the service are certainly appropriate to today's evangelistic endeavors:

"We are so apt to think that this must be done, and that that must be done, and that a certain fixed course of procedure must be followed, or else we must not look for results. Too often, I fear, our rules and regulations and orders of service simply intrude between men's souls and their God. We all need to be taught when to stand aside.

"The figures for the Glasgow campaign do not indicate with anything like completeness the total results. When the ministers of the city came to visit the individual inquirers, they often found that in the same house there were three or four other persons who had been brought to God during the meetings. When a Scotsman is once set on fire he blazes away at white heat. And so it came about that among the best workers during the closing weeks of the mission were the converts of earlier weeks. I have never met people in my life who could sing Sankey's hymns better than the folks of Edinburgh and Glasgow."

The reference to follow-up in the Gipsy's report is interesting since we so often think that organized follow-up is an invention of our own day.

During his stay in Glasgow the Gipsy met many scholars, including Professor Henry Drummond. Like many other learned men, Professor Drummond was very interested in the way that the Gipsy preached. The Gipsy himself considered Professor Drummond a man who conveyed an unmistakable impression of greatness. Dr. Bruce also attended the services and took part in one of them. Talking to his students Dr. Bruce had described the inquiry room as tomfoolery, but he was quick to tell his hearers to hear the Gipsy "because he preaches the gospel."

Was the inquiry room tomfoolery? Certainly many people who entered it became Christians and never went back on their decision. Dr. George Reith, pastor of the Free College Church, wrote an account of the mission for his church's journal:

"We have seen nothing like it since the visit of Moody and Sankey in 1874. The speaking was remarkable. We have seldom, if ever, listened to a long series of addresses of the kind so admirable in every respect—effective, pointed and free from sensational appeals. Our friend Gipsy Smith has left memories of a singularly pleasant kind and, what is more important, his presentation of the gospel of our Lord will not soon be forgotten by those who heard it."

Commenting on the inquiry room, another contributor to the journal wrote:

"Judicious management of the inquiry room is admittedly one of the most difficult and delicate departments of evangelistic work, but we are sure no one who remained to confer with Gipsy Smith would ever regret having done so."

The work done in the inquiry room was simple

enough. Inquirers were pointed to the Saviour through
scripture and then directed to their local church.
Ministers were able to follow up many of these in-
quiries with great effect. That above all must be the
true test of any campaign: did it build up the church?
The Glasgow campaign—called by the *North British
Daily Mail,* "a Glasgow Pentecost"—certainly did that.
It had an encouraging effect in more ways than we
might expect. For example, the sponsors of the campaign would not let Gipsy have a musical instrument
for the morning or afternoon services because, in their
view, the staid, sober and decorous Presbyterians might
regard instrumental music as a desecration of the sanc-
tuary! The Gipsy, whose sense of humor was never far
away when faced with such problems, commented on
this lack of joyful noise during the last service of the
campaign, held at the City Hall.

Looking back on that wonderful campaign, the
Gipsy could later write, "Since 1894 however, things
have greatly changed, even in Scotland, and most of
the Presbyterian churches, I am told, have now or-
gans or harmoniums. I do not believe for a moment
that the result has been a diminution in the solidity and
gravity of the Scottish character."

17

The Miracle of Morchard Bishop

There is something in religion which makes midnight merry and the dark full of song.

The purposes of God run deep, far deeper than any man can comprehend. Let us consider the Gipsy's visit to Australia in 1894. Its success was largely due to Samuel J. Way, the Chief Justice of Australia, and the story of that encounter encompasses the globe.

Many years before, a poor but pious tradesman lived in the small village of Morchard Bishop, on the northern edge of Dartmoor in Devon. He sympathized with the then unpopular work of the Methodist preachers, and often lent them his horse so that they could travel on to preach the gospel. Early in life, the tradesman and his wife died, leaving an orphan son, James. He seems to have possessed some of the carefree attitude of the gypsy for, it is recorded, he used to imitate the Methodist preachers to amuse his friends. He also held mock services—a prophetic act indeed for, as a young lad, he was challenged by a sermon in the parish church. Unfortunately the vicar, though a conscientious man, seemed unable to present a clear plan for salvation. So young James went to one of the evangelical meetings conducted by the vigorous Bible Christian Church and was converted. Like young Gipsy Smith,

James had three books—a hymnbook, a Bible and a biblical dictionary. Soon he became a local preacher and, for some three years, traveled the distances around Dartmoor on horseback or on foot to preach the gospel. On being accepted for the full work of the ministry in 1826, James walked the sixty miles to his appointment to the Weare circuit in Somerset. Like the young Gipsy Smith, he was being called to a greater work than he could perceive.

There was much opposition to the true preaching of the gospel in those days and James had to overcome many difficulties. His life was threatened and, on at least one occasion, he was turned out of the house in which, as a visiting preacher, he was staying.

Characteristic of the devotion of the young preacher was his fifty-mile walk, while in the Brighton circuit, on Britain's southern coastline, to Tenterden, to purchase the nine volumes of Dr. Adam Clarke's *Commentary* for twenty-five dollars (this, by the way, represented almost a third of his annual stipend). The price was half the original cost. Bearing his weighty and valuable purchase, James walked back home.

In 1847, James Way was elected president of the Bible Christian Conference. Then he fell seriously ill. Prayers were said for him and he made a remarkable recovery. Only a little while later James Way volunteered for service in South Australia, as a result of an appeal made at the 1849 conference. The appeal was necessary because of the large number of people who had left Cornwall and Devon to go to the new goldfields in South Australia. James Way was the first man to volunteer. The dedication service, held in the small chapel at Shebbear, was a most moving occasion. Many people wept, believing that they would never see the beloved minister again. The minister's son, Samuel, now fourteen, was to be left behind to continue his studies at the denominational college at Shebbear.

James and his wife arrived in Australia in November, 1850. Over the years and until his death in 1884, the minister was to be a great blessing to the country. He retired from the full-time work of the ministry in 1877 and it was about this time that Samuel, now reunited with his parents (he followed them to Australia some two years after their departure), entered the House of Assembly. A matter of months afterward he became Attorney General and, in 1876, was appointed Chief Justice. Only fifteen years earlier had he been admitted to practice in the Supreme Court of Adelaide: now he held the highest legal office in the land.

Gipsy Smith met Samuel Way in America, probably during Way's visit which embraced, among other things, the great Ecumenical Methodist Conference at Washington in 1891. They shared much in common, for Samuel Way remained an evangelical Christian to the end of his days, loving the simple and sincere fellowship in which he had been reared. So the Gipsy certainly had one good friend in Australia.

He certainly needed a friend or two when he arrived in Adelaide on May 22, 1894. It had been a tiring trip —the Gipsy was never a particularly good sailor and he considered the people on board ship "the most godless set of beings that I have ever mingled with . . . they spent their time in drinking and gambling, and all the forms of worldliness that they could devise." During the voyage, a number of the passengers asked the evangelist to address them, but he suggested that they come to his campaign meetings in Australia instead. He knew that their motives were simply those of curiosity rather than repentance.

The Gipsy's arrival in Adelaide was unpromising. He came unheralded and presented his letters of introduction to the Methodist General Conference. The ministers were not very impressed and asked why they had not been informed that the Gipsy was coming. They did not feel able to arrange a campaign on the spur of the moment. Thomas Cook, the world-famous Wesleyan evangelist, had recently conducted a campaign in Adelaide but had moved on to other engagements. Mr. Cook had planned to take a campaign at Archer Street Church but was now unable to do so. Naturally, the Gipsy offered to fill the gap, but the minister said the people were too disappointed at Mr. Cook's inability to come—and, one way and another, the Methodists felt unable to accept the offer of the Gipsy's services. One can sympathize with their point of view, but the Gipsy announced he was determined to preach in Adelaide, even if it meant preaching in the street. He was able to say, quite truthfully, he knew of a pulpit which was open to him.

Samuel Way was a member of the Franklin Street Bible Christian Church, and so it was that coincidence (if there is such a thing) brought Gipsy into that pulpit. The church held several hundred people and was crowded every night of the Gipsy's ten-day campaign. The wonderful blessings experienced at the church were broadcast all over the city, so that the disappointed congregation at Archer Street became more than willing that the Gipsy should take the place of Mr. Thomas Cook. In all, the evangelist stayed in the city for six weeks, speaking to great congregations, to the convicts (undoubtedly, Samuel Way was instrumental in this), and giving his lecture on his life to a large audience. Incidentally, tickets were sold for the lecture, and the sum of £100 raised for the local children's hospital.

Before the Gipsy left Adelaide he was invited to a farewell breakfast with the Chief Justice. The Gipsy could not attend but he heard from Samuel Way some time later, when the Chief Justice came to England for a short visit. "Your work in Australia will never be forgotten," the Chief Justice said.

Annie, the Gipsy's wife, fell ill during this period. Indeed, some reports in the Australian press, appearing at the end of the evangelist's tour, suggested that the good lady had died. These rumors were untrue. However, the Gipsy labored for three weeks under considerable strain; he could not secure a passage back to England in less than three weeks and so decided to spend a little time with Thomas Cook.

Cook himself was delighted to share the Gipsy's fellowship, since he was involved in a great campaign at Melbourne. A Melbourne newspaper described the day's events thus:

> Gipsy Smith took the morning service to relieve Mr. Cook. The building was quite full, an event which has not happened for many a long year at a morning service. The whole sermon bristled with tersely-put truth, straight home-thrusts and earnest appeals, varied in a most natural and easy manner by irresistible flashes of humour and the tenderest pathos. The description of the punishment of the two boys for playing truant, the callousness of the elder, and the contrition, repentance and forgiveness

of the younger, how he reassured himself again and
again of the fact of his forgiveness, and then
abandoned himself to the enjoyment of the restored
favour of his father, brought tears to almost every
listener. After the sermon, Mr. Smith sang, "Throw
out the lifeline". He has a beautiful voice which,
moderated and controlled by the heart-feeling behind it, finds a response in the hearts of those who
listen which words would fail to elicit. About two
hundred stood for consecration at the close of this
service.

The afternoon meeting was for men only; and a
magnificent sight it was, towards three o'clock, to see
the great building packed with many standing. Gipsy
Smith sang, "The Saviour is my all in all"; and "Onward Christian Soldiers" from the audience was
something to remember. The Rev. Thomas Cook
gave the address, a straight-out piece of personal
dealing from end to end. At the conclusion, Mr.
Smith sang, "Can a boy forget his mother's prayers?"
and eighteen sought and found the Saviour.

At the evening service, the church was filled to
overflowing in every available spot long before the
time of the meeting; so the Conference Hall was
again opened, and soon also crowded out; no more
could be packed in either. Rev. J. W. Tuckfield
opened the Conference Hall meeting, while Gipsy
Smith sang in the church. As soon as this was over
he took charge of the meeting in the Hall, and sang
the same piece again: "Come, the dear Master is
calling".

"God has given every one of you," he said, "a
square chance for heaven. He has called you by a
thousand loving entreaties, by bereavement, by special invitations such as these meetings, and now He
calls you by the lips of a poor gipsy boy, who al-

though he never went to school, has crossed the Jordan and given himself to Christ". At the close of the service, sixteen found the Saviour.

With Thomas Cook's ready cooperation, special noonday services were arranged on three days during the Melbourne campaign. On each day more than two thousand people (mainly men) turned up for the noonday services. On Thursday evening the Gipsy gave the story of his life, by this time one of the world's most famous testimonies. The meeting was due to start at 7:30, but at four o'clock the church was full and about four times as many people were waiting outside. Great crowds awaited the Gipsy wherever he preached now but, going on to Sidney, he received another cablegram referring to his wife's health: "Wife very seriously ill. Come home at once."

Although he had been less than three months in that great continent the Gipsy had taken Australia by storm. Yet, had it not been for his friendship with Chief Justice Way, he might not have preached a single sermon. As the evangelist sailed from Sydney on that June day, as two thousand people waved good-bye, it could have been said of both men, the one a great legal mind, the other still a son of nature: "Seest thou a man diligent in his business? he shall stand before kings; he shall not stand before [obscure] men" (Proverbs 22:29).

18

Bumps and Buffetings

The man in the tomb is a full-length photograph of what the devil would do with every man if he had his way.

Many years after the Gipsy's campaigns in Australia, Billy Graham was to share his sentiments that "there are untold possibilities for Christian work in that country." The Gipsy was the very man to speak to people who, in his estimation, were often homesick. Indeed, the evangelist's comments in his autobiography make interesting reading even now—though that great nation has obviously changed in many respects.

"There are not a few people in Australia," he wrote, "who have been shipped there by their friends in England, so that they may redeem their careers and stand erect on their feet again. Such people gain from their new life not only new opportunities, but fresh susceptibility to moral and religious influences. They make the material among which good evangelistic work can be done. They come to your meetings, and because you are from home, you make a particular appeal to them. You are a link between them and the people they have left behind and they think that you are speaking to them in the name of their friends in the old country. It seemed to me easy to get the Australians to attend

evangelistic services. It fell that my visit immediately
followed their great financial collapse and it may be
that their distress and difficulties made their hearts
more hungry for the gospel."

The Gipsy thought objectively about his campaigns.
Although he took godly advantage of the needs of the
time, he did not regard himself as a man of any importance. "I'm God's messenger from the gypsy tent,"
he would say. "And it's the message that's important,
not the messenger."

The Gipsy stopped at New York on his way home,
there receiving the news that his wife was much better
and that there was no need for him to hurry home if
other work was in hand. So the Gipsy visited Ocean
Grove and conducted a month's campaign in Indianapolis, where he visited the former President of the
United States, Benjamin Harrison. It was in this city
that the Gipsy had an unusual encounter. As he prepared for a meeting one evening, an old minister came
up and placed his hands on the Gipsy's head. Gipsy
Smith thought the old saint was going to pronounce
some kind of benediction but, instead, the stranger felt
the Gipsy's head.

"I'm trying to find your bumps," the old man explained. "So that I can find the secret of your success!"

"Ah, well," smiled the Gipsy. "If you want to find
that, you must come down here!" He placed his hand
upon his heart. "It isn't what's in a man's head that
matters, brother—but what he has in his heart!"

To the end of his ministry the Gipsy was to be
pestered, puzzled and amused by people who wondered as to the Gipsy's secret of success. Maybe they
just did not know their Bibles well enough.

In Indianapolis, too, the Gipsy underwent a minor throat operation and was surprised when the specialist refused a fee.

"Mr. Smith," the specialist said. "Two of my sons have been converted during your services here. How could I ever pay for *that?* I count it a great privilege to help you preach."

So the Gipsy paid by signing his name in the new Bibles which the specialist had purchased for his sons. Then, bumps and all, the Gipsy returned to England. His tour around the world had lasted for eight months: now, after the warmth of welcome and climate he had enjoyed in Australia, he walked ashore in the old country on a cold November morning. But he was glad to be home.

London was waiting for him, however, as he had promised to conduct meetings in the capital on his return from Australia. Indeed, he had assured the then secretary of the London Congregational Union, the Reverend Andrew Mearns, that he would commit three months to work in the metropolis. Mr. B. F. Byrom, who was virtually in charge of the evangelist's itinerary, had been making arrangements for the London campaign and, only a few weeks after the Gipsy's return to England, the two men journeyed to London to finalize the program. However, the Gipsy had hardly arrived in London when he received a telegram urging him to return home as his wife was again seriously ill. The doctors hardly expected Annie to live much beyond the nineteenth of December, 1895, as she had suffered a series of hemorrhages. When they saw the improvement in her condition later on the nineteenth, they declared it a resurrection. It was to be five or six

months before Annie fully recovered from the illness.
The Gipsy regarded the miracle of her recovery as due
to the prayers of his many friends.

He was, of course, reluctant to leave his wife in
January when the London campaign was to begin. But
she was much better and Annie, though dogged by ill-
health throughout her life, always realized the importance of her husband's ministry. So he went to take a
campaign which, in many ways, was almost a failure.

In his own words, the Gipsy was sent "to several
churches which were practically deserted. Indeed, my
work was mostly among weak causes—in a few in-
stances, causes without a pastor or any organized band
of workers. Most of the campaigns were only for a
week. It took one week to make oneself felt in these
localities and just when one was beginning to get a
good hold on these people, one had to leave and go
elsewhere. Good was done, I am sure, and in every
case before the week was finished we had crowded
congregations.

"But it was surely unwise to send me to chapels
which were without pastors, because there was no one
to look after any converts that God gave us. In this
campaign, I worked at ten or eleven places. The right
plan would have been the selection of six or seven of
the strongest churches and a fortnight's mission in
each. In a live church, with a capable minister and a
competent band of workers, something great might
have been accomplished. To send an evangelist to some
deserted, disorganized chapel, situated somewhere perhaps in a godless wilderness, and then expect valuable
results in a week, is like sending a man to gather apples
in the Sahara desert."

However, the Gipsy had great encouragement in the north of England during a week's campaign at Dr. Alexander McLaren's church in Manchester. Initially, the Gipsy had attempted to decline the invitation, feeling that he was unworthy to stand in the pulpit occupied by Dr. McLaren, certainly one of the greatest preachers of the time. The thoroughness with which the campaign was prepared was in contrast to the piecemeal approach of the work at London. Thousands of visits were made by the members of the church to their neighbors and to people throughout Manchester. Thousands of printed invitations were sent out, all of them personally signed by Dr. McLaren and the Reverend J. E. Roberts, the co-pastor. The Gipsy relates that he had a tough time with the evil one during the week before the campaign. The old man told the Gipsy that his methods were certain to fail, since the people who went to Union Chapel were well-educated and cultured. They would certainly learn nothing from a gypsy who had not even gone to school. This struggle with Satan was very real, and continued up to the moment when the evangelist walked to the steps to the pulpit. But he paused at the first step and there committed the meeting to God.

The campaign was a great success. From all over Lancashire, people came to hear the gospel. During those eight days at the Union Chapel, some six hundred people professed to accept Christ; it was, for the Gipsy, one of the most remarkable campaigns of his life. Ministers, hitherto suspicious of the Gipsy's methods, because they did not accept this form of evangelism, began to revise their opinions, for, if people could be simply brought to Christ by a gypsy's preaching in the

Union Chapel of all places, it must be possible anywhere!

Later, when the campaign was over, and its impact could be seen clearly, the co-pastor of Union Chapel was to write, "It is impossible to say how many of the five hundred persons who passed through the inquiry rooms have stood the test of time. They came from every church and chapel in the neighborhood. In our own church, we reaped large results. Many of the converts were gathered into classes, where they were further instructed in the principles of church membership. None were proposed for membership until three months had passed. Then great numbers were added to the church, of whom the large proportion have continued steadfastly in the church doctrine and breaking of bread and prayer. Some of our best workers today were converted under Gipsy Smith."

After some time, in 1895, the Gipsy visited Swansea and sang a verse in Welsh—this he had learned many years before from a young evangelist. The good folk of Swansea were delighted and must have anticipated some good Welsh *hwyl,* a traditional form of fervent preaching in Welsh which is partly chanted or sung.

"Will you be preaching in Welsh?" they asked eagerly.

The Gypsy reflected.

"I think I prefer English," he said finally. Of course, they loved his preaching, but they enjoyed the singing, too.

"It was a wonderful campaign," the Gipsy said. "But my trouble was that once you started those good people singing, you could not stop them."

19

Finding a Wife for Cornelius

When Jesus comes into a life, He sweetens, ennobles, beautifies and transforms it.

The three stalwarts—Cornelius, Woodlock and Bartholomew—continued their own evangelistic work for many years. Gipsy did not see his father as often as he would have liked but, when they were reunited, it was certainly a celebration! Cornelius was still a widower in his forty-ninth year when Gipsy suggested that he marry again. The suggestion took his father by surprise but Gipsy continued his argument by pointing out that Cornelius was still a fit, energetic man, "a good catch." Cornelius seemed quietly pleased at his son's words.

"Well, who would have me, Rodney?" he inquired, half in jest.

"I know just the lady," beamed the evangelist. He went on to explain that during a recent campaign held locally, a widow came around to the vestry after the meeting to inquire of Cornelius' whereabouts. The Gipsy had caught on to this good lady's interest and decided to tease her. When one evening she asked where Cornelius was, Gipsy said, in mock seriousness, "Why? Do you want to buy some clothespins?"

Understandably, the lady was embarrassed. The Gipsy had treated it as a little joke but, in his heart, had later reflected that this would be a good match. Mrs. Sayer, the widow, was an earnest Christian who had been involved in evangelistic work. And she would certainly look after Cornelius well.

When Gipsy had finished his description of Mrs. Sayer's interest and virtues, he could see that his father was very pleased.

"Yes," said Cornelius. "As a matter of fact, I *like* Mrs. Sayer very much."

But it was such a long, long time since Cornelius had married his first wife, Polly, that he was not too sure of the procedure for proposing marriage. In any case he could not write. So it was decided that the Gipsy would compose and dispatch the letter of proposal. The marriage proved to be a very happy one. When Mrs. Sayer became the second Mrs. Cornelius Smith she more than lived up to the Gipsy's expectations. She used to travel about the country with her husband, helping him with his campaigns. Having been a captain in the Salvation Army and, before that, a colporteur in the east end of London, she knew what evangelism was all about. Many people alive today can remember her singing at the meetings conducted by Cornelius.

It was in the year of his marriage to Mrs. Sayer that Cornelius lost his brother, Woodlock. Two years later, Bartholomew died. Gipsy Smith recalled the words of his father: "The Lord knew when He took away my dear brothers that I should feel their loss and feel unfit to go to meetings alone, so my wife was given to me. And the Lord is making us a great blessing. Our time is fully spent in His work and wherever we go, souls are saved and saints are blessed."

It is true, indeed, that Cornelius' second wife was a very unusual woman. The talents for evangelism that she possessed combined with a sweet disposition.

Cornelius certainly knew his New Testament, though it was probably the only book that he ever read. He had a wonderful way of weaving large passages of Scripture, committed to memory into his sermons. When Gipsy Smith conducted a campaign at the Metropolitan Tabernacle, one of London's most famous churches, Cornelius gave a short address on "Christ in us and we in Christ." He said that "some people may think that that is impossible, but it is not. The other day I was walking by the seaside at Cromer and I picked up a bottle with a cork in it. I filled the bottle with salt water and, driving in the cork, I threw the bottle out into the sea as far as my right arm could send it. Turning to my wife I said, 'Look, the sea is in the bottle and the bottle is in the sea. So if we are Christ's, we are in Him and He is in us.'"

Cornelius was a remarkable man. If we ever need any proof of the transforming power of God in a man's life, we need look no further. Cornelius was uneducated but he was wise. Gipsy Smith relates a turning point in his life, by referring to his father's understanding of God's purposes for the boy, Rodney:

"Before my conversion while I was under deep conviction of sin, I used to pray, 'O God, make me a good boy. I want to be a good boy. Make me feel I am saved.' In my young foolishness of heart, I was keen on feeling. My father had heard me pray and had tried to meet my difficulty, without success. However, it chanced that, one afternoon, we were invited to drink tea at the house of a friend in a village where the three brothers were conducting a campaign. Attached to the house was a beautiful large garden, containing many heavily laden cherry trees. My father was as merry and as whole-hearted as a boy and, not ashamed of liking cherries, we all went out to pick the fruit.

"Presently, I was amazed to observe my father gazing up steadfastly at the cherries and saying, in a loud, urgent voice, as he kept the inside pocket of his coat wide open. 'Cherries, come down and fill my pocket! Come down, I say—I want you.' I watched his antics for a moment or two, not knowing what to make of this aberration. At length I said, 'Daddy, it's no use telling the cherries to come down and fill your pocket. You must pluck them off the tree.'

" 'My son,' said my father in pleased and earnest tones, 'That is what I want you to understand. You are making the mistake I was making just now. God has offered you a great gift. You know what it is, and you know that you want it. But you will not reach forth your hand to take it.' "

Cornelius had the instincts of a true preacher. Once he was speaking in the open air at Leytonstone in East London. A vegetable vender passed by and thought that he would make a joke at the preacher's expense.

"Keep at it, old fellow," he shouted. "You'll get half-a-crown for preaching like that!" (A half crown was a coin worth about fifty cents.)

"Not at all," Cornelius replied. "My Master never gives *half* crowns away but only whole ones. The Bible tells us, 'Be thou faithful unto death, and I will give thee a crown of life.' "

The man traveled on; it would be interesting indeed to know of his thoughts at that moment.

A Norwich businessman, George Chamberlain, took a great interest in Cornelius and helped him with his evangelistic work in that area. On one occasion George Chamberlain gave Cornelius a ticket to an exhibition of agricultural machinery, certain that the gypsy would be interested to see the many mechanical wonders. However, when the businessman arrived at the exhibition a little later, he was amazed to find Cornelius preaching from the pulpit of a large piece of equipment. When Cornelius stepped down, his friend inquired what had prompted him to such action, especially as he had not consulted the organizers of the exhibition.

"In all this wonderful exhibition," explained Cornelius, "I did not find one piece of equipment that even claimed to take away the power of sin from men's hearts. Well, *I* know of something that can do this and I thought that all these people should know of it, too."

Looking back on the work of Cornelius and his brothers one is prompted to echo the thoughts of Genesis, "there were giants in the land in those days." These broad men were certainly servants of God. They never lost any opportunity of preaching; you would hear them outside the church building as often as you would hear them inside. Many of the people who traveled miles to hear the converted gypsy brothers were immediately convinced of the power of the gospel, for they had known the trio in earlier times when all three lived unregenerate lives. The meetings were simple enough. Woodlock spoke first—he had taught himself to read and was a man of deep meditation. As the Gipsy wrote of him, "he was very strong and clear on the utter ruin of the heart by the fall, and on redemption by the blood of Christ, our substitute. Over the door of his cottage at Leytonstone he had printed the words, 'When I see the blood, I will pass over.' It was very characteristic."

When Woodlock had spoken, the three brothers sang, Cornelius playing his "hallelujah fiddle." Bartholomew, unable to read, learned many texts, aided by his wife. He gave a personal testimony, interspersed with a few of these texts. Cornelius spoke last and he gathered up, as it were, all that had gone before in the meeting and spoke earnestly to the congregation. Like Gipsy himself, Cornelius had the power to move his audience to tears—not deliberately, but in the simple recitation of the gospel message.

The three brothers loved to travel the country, preaching the message. When Cornelius married for the second time, Gipsy pointed out that he would have to establish a proper home. Cornelius, a true gypsy, was aghast at the suggestion that he buy land and build on it, but was finally convinced of the necessity for it. Buying land at Leytonstone, the brothers built three wooden cottages—but they stood them on wheels. This, at least, gave them the illusion of being able to move on!

Woodlock had a special burden to carry, in the person of a nonchristian wife. He knew that he would have to suffer ridicule from his wife whenever he returned from a meeting. But, as soon as she had finished giving him her opinion on his preaching, he would suggest that they sing a verse and would strike up "My Jesus, I Love Thee," or some similar piece—his wife never joined in.

He died as the result of an accident in March, 1882, the first of the brothers, as Gipsy put it, "to go home."

Following a meeting he rushed from the church to catch up with his brothers as they were to catch a train. In the darkness, Woodlock struck a post and suffered considerable injuries. He died in his home a day later and more than fifty gypsies came to the funeral at Leytonstone churchyard. There were more than four hundred friends and relatives, too. Such was the character of this remarkable man, still below fifty years of age when he died.

Bartholomew died only two years later, following a protracted illness. His wife, who was expecting a child, was prostrate with grief but Cornelius urged her to pray that her heavenly Father's will be done. She did so and a great peace came upon her and the room. It may seem melodramatic to pen such a phrase today, but it was certainly their experience: sweet indeed is the departing of the saints.

Cornelius lived on for many more years, "like a tree planted by the rivers of water" in Gipsy's words. Often Cornelius and his son talked about the wonderful times of blessing they had enjoyed in the past and of all the amazing experiences they had shared since Polly's death, all those years before.

20

We Have Seen Strange Things Today

If Jesus takes possession of you, you too will be attractive. Your life will become Christ over again to someone else.

The Gipsy conducted the last campaign of 1895 in Edinburgh, Scotland, where, according to the *British Weekly,* "great crowds gathered to hear the Gipsy preach and sing. All who have been associated with him will bear grateful testimony to his marvellous success. His remarkable testimony contributes not a little to this result. There is a romance associated with his name and history. His gift of song also adds greatly to the charm and fascination . . . his bright, hearty, happy Christian spirit has strikingly conveyed his gospel message, and conveyed the marked and unmistakable impression of a true evangelist endued with rare spiritual power." It is true that some newspaper reports tended to center on the singer, not the song. The Gipsy himself much preferred the press to reprint part, if not all, of the text of his message to reach those who thought it was too chilly to leave the fireside. But those were days before the widespread press exploitation of personalities that we know today. The Gipsy was always good for a news story and editors tended to be over-generous in the space they allocated to the speaker himself.

When the Gipsy sailed for New York on New Year's Day, 1896, he was going to conduct one of his most important campaigns. There was but one engagement in his diary and that was at the People's Temple at Boston, then the city's largest Protestant church. There was seating accommodation for between twenty-five hundred and three thousand people, the higher figure including school premises which could be opened up, if necessary. Dr. James Boyd Brady, the pastor of this impressive church, had invited the Gipsy to Boston, and both men had been praying for a great work. Indeed, the possibilities of revival were the very reason why the Gipsy had kept his diary free from other engagements. Here too, however, the publicity end of the arrangements tended to overstate the Gipsy's endowments. As he passed the People's Temple, on his way to Dr. Brady's home, the Gipsy noticed a great sign outside the church:

GIPSY SMITH, THE GREATEST EVANGELIST
IN THE WORLD

"God doesn't send revival in order that we can take the glory for ourselves," he commented and, at the very first opportunity, requested that the sign be taken down. As he told the congregation during the first evening of the campaign, "I do not feel that I am the greatest evangelist in the world and you do not believe it." Of course, many members of the congregation had not been sure what to believe about their guest. Some seemed to think that he might turn up in full Romany regalia, gypsy wagon and all. The Boston papers threw overboard any restraint they might have had, and described the Gipsy as "a spiritual phenomenon, an intellectual prodigy, and a musical and oratorical paragon." "Fame," as the Gipsy said, "could be the evangelist's greatest burden; one could only ignore it, and point people to Christ."

The campaign shook Boston. There was a sense of revival in the air. On the morning after the opening meeting an agitated man called to see the evangelist, who was roused from his slumbers. The visitor was brought to the Gipsy's room. "Can't you leave me alone?" he declared. "Why did you follow me all the way to Boston?"

The somewhat wild-eyed caller proved to be a man from Hanley who, years before, had heard the Gipsy preach on many occasions, but who had rejected the message. Since that time he had deserted his family and come to America, where he now lived a sinful and confused existence. Occasionally stricken by remorse he had written to his wife in England but never received any reply. Indeed, he did not know whether his wife and children were alive or dead.

In the midst of this depravity and despair he had bought a newspaper which stabbed his conscience further by its report of Gipsy Smith's arrival in the city. His motives for coming to see the evangelist must have been mixed indeed; somewhere, deep in that darkened heart, he must have known that the burden he now carried came from his rejection of the Gipsy's message those years before. As the visitor told his story and gradually relaxed, the Gipsy paid careful attention to all the details. He still had many friends in

Hanley and the potteries, and believed that he might be able to trace the family which this man had abandoned. But first, the man must be brought to himself. The Gipsy spoke to him about the old days in Hanley, and of the message of salvation. He told his visitor that nothing could be done until the man truly repented and came to Christ. Thoughtfully and sorrowfully the man went away, and the Gipsy returned to his much-needed rest. The visitor had promised to come to the very next meeting at the People's Temple and the Gipsy watched closely for him. Sure enough, the man was among those who came forward to give their lives to the Saviour. It was a genuine conversion; the man truly did become a new creation in Christ. The Gipsy wrote to his brother-in-law, Councilor Ball of Hanley, giving him full details of the lost family. With the aid of the local press and the police, the wife and children were found and, soon afterward, they crossed the Atlantic to be reunited with the husband and father. They became active Christians, living a fruitful and happy life. The Gipsy, when telling the end of this story, beamed, "Well, that was worth getting up early for!"

Such encounters were not unusual in the Gipsy's life. Although he was a public figure and almost always surrounded by people, he often stopped to help the individual. The Gipsy obviously became caught up with the sense of revival at Boston. He related some of the experiences in his autobiography:

"One night, going to church, I jumped into a tram. Sitting beside me was a lady with a pair of opera glasses in her hand. She was not going to church. People do not take opera glasses to church. I suppose they think they see enough of the parson without them. Presently, a lady on her way to my meeting entered the car and said to me, 'What are you going to preach about tonight, Mr. Smith?' 'Wait and see,' I answered. If you tell the people what you are going to talk about they can fortify themselves. Glorious surprises are what we need in our preaching more and more. Some people will never be saved unless they are taken off their guard. However, I said to my questioner, 'We shall have nearly three thousand people tonight and whether we preach or not, we shall certainly pray. And the burden of our prayer will be, 'O, Lord, send down upon us the Holy Spirit.' 'Sir, sir,' said the lady with the opera glasses, 'Are you not afraid that something will happen if you pray like that?' 'Oh, not at all,' I said. 'Not *afraid*—we hope something will happen. We are going to church because we expect something will happen.' "

And it did. The campaign, originally intended to last for four weeks, ran into seven. Night after night, crowds of people came to hear the Gipsy. Night after night, hundreds came forward to the communion rail. On the fifth Sunday the Gipsy gave a sermon on the text "Be filled with the Spirit," and a great silence fell upon the congregation. When the Gipsy had finished speaking there was a pause, and then the pastor of the church, Dr. James Boyd Brady, stood up.

"I feel the need of that experience of which our brother has been speaking," the pastor said. "I am going down to the communion rail to seek that personal Pentecost for myself. I shall never be able to care for the young souls that have been brought to God during this campaign unless I am filled with the Holy Spirit."

He walked slowly to the communion rail and knelt in prayer. In silence, between two and three hundred other people joined the pastor at the front of the church, where Gipsy led them in a short prayer of dedication.

"We all felt that we had seen strange things that day," the Gipsy said later.

It had not been a fervent service, full of emotion. Indeed, there was an awe about the sense of dedication (and rededication) that no man could himself generate. Later, the Gipsy was asked if he would succeed to the pastorate of the People's Temple, since Dr. Boyd Brady was soon to retire. But the evangelist said no courteously and simply, explaining that his calling was that of evangelist rather than of pastor. Throughout those years the Gipsy was being invited to this or that position or pastorate. If, as so many of his critics have said, he was in it for the money, he could have found a comfortable position easily enough and avoided all those ocean voyages which he *never* enjoyed. As a result of the campaign at Boston some eight hundred people were received into the church on probation.

While in Boston the Gipsy talked to the students of the Methodist College on how to win souls, a talk which he also gave to the students of Harvard University. As Dr. Billy Graham has discovered in our own times, students were not so much interested in intellectual fireworks—the Gipsy could not provide those —as in hard facts about the gospel in action. The Gipsy had a natural gift for talking to people as man to man and he certainly won the respect of the students who heard him.

After one such gathering the Gipsy commented that

he would dearly love to take a year off to study. A minister friend smiled and said, "But that would only spoil you, Gipsy!"

Washington, D.C., also gave the Gipsy a warm welcome. He conducted a campaign at the Metropolitan Episcopal Church, where Dr. Hugh Johnstone was pastor. A member of the church was Dr. Milburn, the chaplain to the Senate. In fact, many Methodist Congressmen attended the church regularly so the Gipsy made plenty of influential friends. Although there is no record that they invited him to run for Congress, the Americans would dearly have kept the gypsy evangelist on their side of the Atlantic. Dr. Milburn, then blind, was an amazing man. He had been chaplain to the Senate for some sixty years. This had started, so the Gipsy related when, as a young man, Dr. Milburn had been preaching in the far West and was on his way home on one of the river steamers. The passengers included a number of Senators and members of the House of Representatives, men who spent their time (on the boat, at least) in gambling, drinking, and swearing. Dr. Milburn was invited to conduct a service in the saloon on Sunday morning and these Congressmen were among the congregation. True to his calling, though not without a certain nervousness, Dr. Milburn rebuked these leaders of the nation for not setting a better example. Then he went into his cabin expecting anything to happen. But, instead of the expected cloudburst, the congressmen came to apologize and asked if they might nominate him as chaplain to the Senate.

It was a good story that Dr. Milburn told and the Gipsy enjoyed every minute of it.

"That's what I tell my young minister friends," the

Gipsy declared. "When you speak for the Lord, you don't have to worry what *men* say!"

He and Dr. Milburn became very good friends. When, during the course of an address, the Gipsy mentioned that he had never been ordained, the old man stood up and placed his hands on the evangelist's shoulders. "Then it is my privilege to ordain you— without a question," he said.

It was a moment that both men remembered with affection and gratitude. "When I count up those things that the ministry has cost me," the Gipsy said, "they are a light burden compared with all the blessings that God has bestowed upon me. And among the greatest of all these blessings are those friends whom I have in many lands. What a reunion there'll be when we all get to heaven!"

21

Into the Twentieth Century

More brilliant than the sun, more bright than the lightning, more beautiful than the songs of all the birds, sounds forth "Him that cometh unto me I will in no wise cast out."

Before leaving America the Gipsy met two very eminent people—the President, Grover Cleveland, and the famous hymn writer, Fanny Crosby (often called by her married name, Mrs. F. J. Alstyne, in the hymn books). The President had a brief but interesting conversation with the evangelist but said that the pressure of his many engagements made it impossible to come to the Gipsy's forthcoming lecture on his life. By this time, the story of his life was one of the highlights of any campaign conducted by Gipsy Smith, and we can only regret that it was never recorded in sound. Fanny Crosby was seventy years of age when Gipsy met her in New York. A small woman, and blind, she was still a great encourager of those active in the work of evangelism. She came to one of the Gipsy's meetings and sat on the platform, listening to every word. It gave the Gipsy great pleasure to sing one of her hymns:

Like a bird on the deep, far away from its nest,
I wandered, my Saviour, from Thee,

But Thy dear loving voice called me home to Thy
  breast,
And I knew there was welcome for me.

Fanny Crosby told the Gipsy that she had never
realized there was so much in that song. Speaking of
her blindness, she added, "I would not see with these
natural eyes if I might, because I should miss much
that I already see."

Over the years the Gipsy collected a repertoire of
songs that would move even the most hardened soul.
Once, while conducting a campaign in Taunton, Somerset, a little girl sang a solo especially for him. It happened during the Gipsy's visit to the local infirmary
and the little girl's song was "Count Your Blessings."
The words of the song impressed the evangelist and he
said that he often forgot to count his blessings. The
sick but cheerful folk he met at the infirmary were
glad to see the Gipsy. He, in turn, counted his blessings—the robust health that God had given to him
and the many talents he possessed in reaching the people. After that he often sang "Count Your Blessings"
at his meetings and told his hearers about the little
girl at Taunton, who had brought *him* a message. It
was, indeed, the most popular song in London during
the evangelist's visit to the Metropolitan Tabernacle in
1900. The Gipsy reported: "wherever one might go—
in the streets, in the trams, in the trains—someone was
humming or whistling 'Count Your Blessings.' The boys
pushing their barrows along, the men driving their
horses, and the women rocking their cradles—all had
been caught by the truth and melody of the hymn."

Many will recall a similar phenomenon during the
early Billy Graham Crusades in London when strains

of "Blessed Assurance" wafted along the passageways of the London Underground.

In the closing years of the nineteenth century Gipsy Smith was the official Free Church evangelist, appointed by the National Free Church Council. In accepting the appointment, the Gipsy thought that it would "do more to break down local prejudices and to bring Christians and churches together than anything done for ages." It seems certain that the Reverend Thomas Law, secretary to the council, was the real mover of the Gipsy's appointment. Although he remained in the background, Mr. Law did much to help the work of the Gipsy in his years as Free Church evangelist. For example, he planned the campaigns and took much of the burden of organization from the Gipsy's shoulders.

It was the Council which published the Gipsy's life-story in 1901, bringing that amazing testimony to a new, great audience. Gipsy Smith started his work for the Council in September, 1897, and was glad for the opportunity to work on home ground for a while. He traveled all around England but resisted calls to conduct campaigns abroad (Americans, by this time, were always very pleased to secure the Gipsy's services).

The last campaign of the nineteenth century was held at Luton, Bedfordshire, at the chapel now used as the headquarters of the Methodist Industrial Mission. It was an amazing campaign. Nearly eleven hundred people came forward as inquirers—more than one-fortieth of the town's population!

"No one ever asks where the converts are," said the Reverend W. H. Thompson, the Wesleyan minister. "They can be seen in every department of our church life. Never before have I been involved in a campaign that left such a bumper crop of converts!"

But, amid all those people, one caught the Gipsy's attention most. His sister, Mrs. Lovinia Oakley, had fallen away from the Christian life. The Gipsy, not mincing words, called her a backslider. But during the campaign she came forward to renew her allegiance to Christ.

The Gipsy's brother-in-law, Mr. Evens, conducted the overflow meetings. On Saturday morning, the two evangelists went to Baldock, to Norton Lane, where Polly (Gipsy's mother) had died, many years before. The two men followed the route of that nocturnal funeral and, as they stood by the unmarked grave, the Gipsy said that he would erect a stone there.

On Monday evening the Gipsy told the story of his life and, at the point where he referred to his mother's death, the Mayor of Luton turned to Mr. Evens and asked if a stone stood at the grave. On hearing that no stone stood there the Mayor said he would insure that one was erected. He was as good as his word. The Gipsy, reflecting that the Mayor had known nothing of the evangelist's own intention of erecting a stone, thought the event a remarkable fulfillment of the verse, "Before they call, I will answer and while they are yet speaking, I will hear" (Isaiah 65:24).

The new century began in a spirit of great hope. A great campaign was planned for London, the provinces, and the countryside, a sequence of planned evangelism to arouse the nation. This massive program lasted from mid-January to early March, and Cornelius was not going to be left out. The fortnight's campaign at the Metropolitan Tabernacle was the zenith of the old man's life. Nor was Cornelius the only relative present. Scores of relatives, many of them strangers to the Gipsy, came to hear him. More than twelve hundred inquirers came forward at the Metropolitan Tabernacle and, every night, Cornelius came along, ready to add his own testimony to his son's preaching of the gospel. Cornelius was also active in the inquiry rooms, assuming a type of unofficial control.

Writing some eight months after the campaign, the Reverend Thomas Spurgeon (then pastor of the Metropolitan Tabernacle) reported "converts resulting from Gipsy Smith's campaign are still appearing and asking to be united with God's people. Those who have already joined us seem to be of the right sort, and these later applicants are bright examples of Christ's power to keep and save . . . I can only confirm my original verdict of it [the campaign] . . . full of real power and blessing."

Dr. Monro Gibson reported the campaign meetings held at Marylebone in northwest London for the *British Weekly,* and added an interesting description of the evangelist himself:

> There is a charm about Gipsy Smith's personality which wins from the outset, and prepares for that response to his earnest appeals which has been marked in every service. He is more expository than any other evangelist whom I have ever heard, and neither his exegesis nor his theology would do discredit to a graduate of our theological schools.
>
> There is an air of culture, even in style, which is nothing less than marvellous to those who know the story of his life, and of which I cannot give any other explanation than that he is a graduate of that

same school which prepared John the fisherman for his literary work. But the great factor is the power from on high with which he speaks and which, manifest the first evening, was increasingly so as the days passed on.

Dr. Clifford, reporting the nearby Paddington campaign for another Christian paper, gave a few additional flourishes to the portrait of the preacher:

His methods are as sane as his Gospel is clear. He has no fads. He is not the victim of vagaries. He knows his work and does it. He does not quarrel with pastors and call it preaching the Gospel. He is their helper. Exhaustless resources of pathos are his. There is a tear in his voice. He moves the heart of his audience to its utmost depths. But he never forgets that a man has an intellect, and thinks and reasons; and when the hearer is most roused "to cross the Rubicon", he holds him in thought as to the meaning of the step he is taking, tells him that going into the inquiry room—important as that is as a definite and distinct choice of discipleship to Christ—is only a beginning, and must be followed by a resolute, patient and thoroughgoing obedience to Christ. His humour is irresistible.

It is one of the sources of his power, for humour is human. . . . He despises conventionality and is as incapable of dullness as he is of obscurity. . . . The ethical rings out in his teaching with terrible resonance. Most of his strength is derived from the directness of his appeals to the conscience. He searches the heart, expresses the subtle devices with which we shirk our responsibilities as Christians, and compels us secretly to admit, if not to confess, our sins. The value of his mission to the avowed disciples of

Christ is not less than to those who are constrained to make the great decision.

But, as the Reverend J. H. Jowett (another great preacher of the age) was to write of the Birmingham campaign held during the year when fifteen hundred people came into the inquiry rooms: "In the Gipsy's heart there dwelt the quietness which is the fruit of a steady faith in the Lord." He added, "in the final appeals, the missioner himself was overlooked in the mighty sense of the presence of God."

That was surely the secret of the unusual ministry of Gipsy Smith. He had a striking personality; you could never forget having met him, just as you could not resist listening to him. But he brought people to that point where they were no longer conscious of the preacher, but only of that mighty power of God which commands men everywhere to repentance. Certainly there is no other way of explaining the many conversions that lasted over decades in every nation which the Gipsy visited.

22

Harvest at Cape Town

Do not put a badge on yourself. Away with your little paint brushes—we know when God paints you within.

Gipsy Smith called his six months in South Africa during 1904, "one of the most surprising periods of my life." The book which he wrote, *A Mission of Peace,* was well named. Going to South Africa so soon after the Boer War, he faced the prospect of Dutch and English churches no longer in communion with another. Nevertheless, he was able to look back and regard the mission as a divine arrangement. In *A Mission of Peace,* he wrote, "from the first day of the first mission in Cape Town to the last in Port Elizabeth, not a hitch, not a cross word, no unpleasantness in any committee or with any particular worker. . . . Every man, from first to last, seemed to forget self and lay his all at the feet of Christ and the service of his brother."

The work of Gipsy Smith there began when the churches in South Africa tried to pick up the pieces at the end of the war. They decided that some new evangelistic vision was needed and sent a petition to the National Free Church Council in England, requesting the Gipsy's services for six months. As this petition came from English Protestant brethren clearly in need, it was received sympathetically—but there were problems. Characteristically, the Gipsy was ready to pack and depart, but knew well enough that much of the seed would fall on thorny ground. "The war," he said, "had left behind it bitterness, hatred, hardness, indifference, sin and scores and hundreds of backsliders. The religious life had nearly been crushed out. Altogether, the state of things was most discouraging."

The Reverend Thomas Law, in charge of the Gipsy's arrangements, hesitated to let the Gipsy leave Britain at that time. The work seemed to be gathering momentum and churches up and down the land were eager to secure the Gipsy's services. So he offered another evangelist to the brethren in South Africa. But they proved adamant.

"We have prayed for guidance," they declared. "God has promised an increase, but we must have Gipsy Smith."

And so the Gipsy went, accompanied by his wife and daughter Zillah, who was to act as soloist. Although he was now living in a comfortable house at Cambridge, Romany Tan, a home which was to become as famous as any in England, the evangelist still regarded Hanley as a second home. His good friends there organized a farewell meeting at the Victoria Hall where Gipsy was the guest of honor. It was a very warm and simple affair, just like the departure of a dear son—and the building was packed. Other farewell meetings were held at Leeds and in London, with a final send-off at the National Free Church Annual Conference at Newcastle-on-Tyne. In addition to all this, large crowds came to Southampton to wish the Gipsy and his family Godspeed. About fifteen hundred people stood on the shore while the Gipsy and his family waved from the deck of the RMS *Saxon*. The crowd sang many of the Gipsy's favorite songs—"Count Your Blessings," "Showers of Blessing," "God Be With You Till We Meet Again"—and then the ship slowly pulled away into deeper waters.

"If all these people keep their promise to pray for me," the Gipsy said, "we shall certainly see revival in South Africa."

The journey was far more successful, from the evangelist's point of view, than that disappointing trip to Australia. Crew and passengers alike were courteous and friendly to the Gipsy, as if the evangelist's presence was an encouragement to them, rather than a judgment! He preached at the ship's services, held both Sundays of the voyage, and almost everyone on board came to hear him. Never a good sailor, the Gipsy could hardly keep his feet that second Sunday, because the ship was rolling so much.

On seeing Cape Town for the first time he thought it magnificent and remarked that he had never seen anything more beautiful. His comments on the populace were less flattering. He thought the people of Cape Town were "made up of thousands of white people, British and Dutch, and thousands of colored of all shades. These, for years, have had one overwhelming passion—the making of money. Money and pleasure, drink, gambling and lust stand out large in the lives of thousands of men in Cape Town and, I think it is safe to say, all over the country. The churches were largely divided, on one side stood the British, on the other side the Dutch. . . . I early saw that the racial difficulty was a big one. Patience, wisdom and a deep spiritual revival in all the churches would be needed in order to bring these people together into one Christian whole."

Although the Gipsy and his family were given a very warm welcome by many Christian leaders, that welcome was not unanimous. For example, as no building in the town was large enough to accommodate the campaign, use of the Dutch Reformed Church was sought. The request was rejected, promptly and curtly. At the time, the town hall had not been completed so, in the end, the organizing committee had to rent an old and somewhat derelict corrugated iron building. Someone said that it was "consecrated" iron rather than corrugated iron! "Well," the Gipsy smiled. "We shall certainly consecrate it!"

The committee spent a considerable sum putting the building in order. Within a remarkably short time the building was ready and topped with a banner bearing the name of the evangelist. Two of the carpenters employed in the building asked the evangelist if they could have "free tickets for the circus."

"Hmmm," mused the Gipsy. "It's just like being back at Hanley." He was recalling his very first campaign held, you recall, in an old circus ring. He told the carpenters that, if they mentioned his name at the door, they would secure front seats. They came, got the front seats—and a blessing, too.

From the very first night the building was packed to capacity, the men outnumbering the women by about eight to one. The audience was certainly multiracial. "It was a sight to witness," the Gipsy wrote, "white and black, rich and poor, British and Dutch, Episcopal and Nonconformist sitting side by side, and here and there one could see a Malay, with his fez in his hand, listening like the rest. There was no difference—all had sinned and Christ is the Saviour of all."

Certainly a spirit of reconciliation sprang from the campaign. Men brought to Christ at the same time and the same place found it hard to erect barriers to fellowship, one with another. In addition, the Gipsy invited ministers to the platform, even those who had not been whole-heartedly behind the campaign at the beginning. It is hardly surprising that he began to make many friends in the Dutch Reformed Church. One of these, Professor Hofmeyer, invited the evangelist to speak to the students at the Theological Seminary at Stellenbosch. This was a great opportunity since the Dutch Reformed Church students had not spoken to the English since the war. The students asked him many searching questions, including what he meant by the reconciliation of Christians.

"Our nations have fallen out," the Gipsy replied. "And it's the duty of Christians in both our lands to give a lead. We have to forgive and forget, and give opportunities for meeting together in fellowship. If we Christians give a lead, the politicians will follow."

Then he added a more personal answer to the question, one which challenged all present (as, indeed, it challenges us, years later). "Suppose we got to heaven, leaving behind a sore spot we could have healed, but *didn't*. We would not like to hear Jesus say, 'You were in that place and you failed to heal that sore spot.' We are all responsible for reconciliation, my friends, and it is an everyday task."

The students were silent. There were many sore spots needing healing in South Africa, that year of 1904.

Stories abound of conversions in the Cape Town campaign. "Backsliders by the score were restored," the Gipsy reported, and added that Cape Town and South Africa represented a "dumping ground for backsliders." In all, more than three thousand people came into the inquiry rooms. Two thousand came to a converts' meeting. Churches and congregations everywhere were revived and refreshed. Someone started wearing a badge of red and white ribbon to symbolize the text. "Though your sins be as scarlet, they shall be as white as snow." Soon, many of the converts wore these badges and, when the Gipsy said goodbye to Cape Town on May 10th, he could see hundreds of these badges in the vast crowd at the railway station.

"It's just like a harvest," he said, tears running down his cheeks. "It's just like a harvest."

23

Vote for Gipsy Smith— and No Beer

You cannot know Christ through your head. You know Him from experience within. You do not take this on—you take this in.

As the spirit of revival swept across South Africa, the Gipsy, who had seen many remarkable sights in his time, was sometimes amazed. He stopped in Wellington for one night, as the guest of Dr. Andrew Murray, and preached to a congregation of fifteen hundred people, mainly young men and women. When the Gipsy made his appeal, about a tenth of the congregation went forward into the inquiry room.

"It seemed as though heaven was very near," the evangelist said later. "Old and young experienced a joy on earth that no words can describe!"

For ten successive nights after the Gipsy's departure, church meetings were held for inquirers—and all as the result of a single sermon!

Kimberley, the "diamond city," was next and, in addition to preaching to the usual large audiences, the Gipsy sang "Count Your Blessings" to several hundred Kaffirs at a compound. Zillah joined her father in the song, and one of the natives interpreted the words for his brethren. During the final meeting at Kimberley,

the Gipsy conducted an interesting experiment. He had
long realized that many converts did not go forward to
the inquiry room, even though they had truly accepted
Christ. He asked such people to stand as an acknowl-
edgement of their decision. Some hundred and fifty
people rose to their feet.

"You see that?" the evangelist beamed to one of the
ministers on the platform, "just think of all the converts we know nothing about!" But the Lord knew
about them!

Even Dutch people who knew little or no English
came to Christ at the Gipsy's meetings—as at Bloem-
fontein, for example, where the evangelist had tea with
the bishop, dean, clergy and Roman Catholic priest.
The local press, here as elsewhere, took a keen interest
in the campaign and considerable correspondence was
given over to the subject of sudden conversion. One of
the campaign's champions was a Roman Catholic priest,
again indicating the Gipsy's power to cross denominational barriers.

The Gipsy's party arrived in Johannesburg on June
9, for a big tent campaign. The tent, capable of seating 3,000 people, had been specially ordered from
England. Two smaller tents were used as inquiry rooms.

"Well, I was born in a tent," smiled the Gipsy, gazing across the vast seating area. "But I think it was a
sight smaller than this."

As it was, they needed every seat. The Johannesburg
tent campaign was probably the most memorable of
all the campaigns of 1904. The evangelist himself was
in no mood for compromise; he made a few enemies,
inevitably. "The Lord was with my word, and unconverted and backsliders knew it; no compromise for sin

or wrong in any shape or form; I tried to hit out everywhere . . . I never felt greater liberty in preaching, and never felt more sure that the Word was in the demonstration of the Spirit and with power. The campaign was the talk of the city—the papers spoke of it fairly well until I said some plain things about the card playing, dancing and the theatre. Then they howled with rage and said my statements were scandalous."

As could be expected, the controversy merely added to the crowds. Some came to ridicule, and were converted. Others came out of curiosity, and were converted. One man was converted as he passed the tent, overhearing just part of the Gipsy's address. Another man, found in a state of neglect, was brought to Christ by one of the campaign workers, who proved to be a Samaritan indeed when he took the stranger into his own home. In all, three thousand people passed through the inquiry tents, and many of them proved to be people from the right side of the tracks. The Gipsy stated that he spoke to many well-to-do people, eager to live a life of reality.

After all that hard work, the evangelist planned a short rest with his family at Pietersburg, two hundred miles up country. But, as soon as he had unpacked his suitcases, he was met by requests to preach at local churches. As usual, he could not refuse.

The Johannesburg tent was next pitched at Pretoria, and another campaign conducted before the Gipsy moved on to Durban, the "garden of South Africa." Natal, the evangelist's next stop on this whirlwind tour, appealed to his great love of nature.

Its "deep valleys; wild rocky ravines; high and often table-topped hills and mountains; its beautiful rivers;

its picturesque waterfalls; and, in summer, its many
wild flowers; its sugar, banana and pineapple planta-
tions; its orange, lemon and naartje groves, and many
other tropical flowers and fruits—all delight the lover
of natural beauty."

It was just as well that the Gipsy was cheered by the
scenery for, at Pietermaritzburg, the capital of Natal, he
met with the most bitter opposition from the people in
the liquor, theatrical and gambling circles. Newspapers
called him a fraud, "king of bunkum" and other un-
flattering titles. Meeting the campaign workers, the
Gipsy attempted to reassure them, though with what
success he was unable to ascertain. "Just trust God for
great things," he told them.

The opening meeting on the Sunday afternoon
brought a great crowd, nearly all men. But the atmosphere was icy, the congregation unresponsive. Yet the
ice melted as the Gipsy preached. In all, about a thousand people came to the inquiry room during the
course of the work at Pietermaritzburg. The Gipsy even
earned some grudging praise from the newspaper. But
the comment which pleased him most was one scrawled
in chalk near the door of his residence: "Keep away
from this man—he is dangerous." As an afterthought,
someone else had chalked "Vote for Gipsy Smith—and
no beer."

24

Ten Minutes Ahead of the Devil

Sin must be something dreadful when only the red fingers of the crucified Christ can remove it..

As the campaign moved on toward the final meetings at Port Elizabeth, Gipsy Smith spent time with the ministers and pastors—those who would be responsible for caring for the many new converts.

"Oh, to preach the old gospel story more and more, in all its fullness, grandeur and eternity, in all the power of the Holy Spirit," he cried. "Do we live to think and pray and work, to focus everything, every thought, power and desire, to bring men to Jesus Christ?"

It rained heavily on Sunday, August 21, the opening day of his campaign in East London. The area around the town hall became a sea of umbrellas as the people waited patiently to enter the building. The Gipsy's text for that opening meeting was simple enough, as was the exposition: "What must I do to be saved?" Coming forward by the hundreds, the good people of East London showed that the Gipsy's expectations for revival were to be confirmed. And so the campaign rolled on. Naturally, there were some surprises, like the curate

who came and asked the Gipsy how to conduct a
prayer meeting; like the young man from Bromley,
Kent, whose sister (converted at one of the Gipsy's
campaigns in England) had witnessed to him with no
effect, but now he accepted Christ; like the town
drunkard, a confirmed alcoholic for twenty years, who
started in sainthood by going forward at the meeting.
They wanted the Gipsy to stay longer, but it was impossible.

"Keep the flame burning," he told them, "and God
will give you evangelists of your own!"

Although he sometimes felt tired, the Gipsy kept
remarkably fit during the entire tour. It was hard
work, but it was work that kept him happy!

The final campaign, held at Port Elizabeth, closed
this wonderful period in the Gipsy's life. The Feather
Market Hall was one of the largest buildings in South
Africa, and it was certainly the largest used in the
campaign. The weather was stormy on that opening
Sunday too, with rain falling in torrents. The people
came by the hundreds, and the building (which was
not at all suitable for the purpose of evangelism) was
soon packed. Two of the ministers working at the
campaign were men who had been converted many
years before, under the ministry of Cornelius, the
Gipsy's father.

"Well, well," the evangelist beamed. "Some people
tell me that conversions do not last and here I find
two that have traveled six thousand miles without any
sign of wearing out!"

Many people came forward at the Port Elizabeth
campaign. The editor of the city's leading newspaper
told the Gipsy that the whole attitude of the area had

changed from indifference and criticism to inquiry and sympathy.

It was as if the evangelist had come to prove the truth of the gospel and its enduring power to save, good news to people who felt that the old beliefs, like so much else, had been shattered by the war. People traveled miles to hear him, were converted, and then returned home, unknown saints in small corners of the kingdom of God. A thousand people passed through the inquiry rooms. On Tuesday, September 13, the organizers held a final praise meeting, in which ministers expressed what the campaign had done for them. One announced that a hundred and twenty people had asked to join his church. Another confessed that he had been renewed spiritually—"My people have a new pastor and it's me!"

The Gipsy and his family took a short holiday in Cape Town before returning to England though, here too, people were eager to talk to him, and to tell him of the continuing revival in their churches. With his friends, Mr. W. Cuthbert, President of the YMCA in South Africa, and his family, the Gipsy managed to find seclusion by climbing to the top of Table Mountain. "It was," he reflected later, "impossible to describe the beauty and grandeur of the scenery."

He came down from that mountaintop to experience another meeting, his final in South Africa. Two hours before the meeting was due to start, crowds were waiting to enter the building. Then, when it began, representatives from the many churches which had heard the Gipsy gave their reports of continuing blessing.

As so often happened during his fast-moving life, the Gipsy faced an impromptu meeting at the dock, as he and his family boarded the ship which was to take them home. Many mission hymns were sung and pocket handkerchiefs waved—then cries of "God bless you" and "Come back soon," as the ship's horn sounded. The ship's band struck up "Auld Lang Syne" as the vessel began to pull away. It was more than the Gipsy could bear. He gave one final wave, and went below to thank God in the quietness of his cabin.

Well, was it real revival or just a spontaneous excitement, transient and soon to fade? We must remember that this was a year of revival in many places, including Britain itself. What really happened in South Africa was just part of a movement which brought blessing to many parts of the world. Had the Gipsy been confronted then by any doubting Thomas, he would have pointed first to the promises of Scripture and then to the prayers of the people.

"Gipsy Smith doesn't matter. If you claim the promises and pray from your heart for revival, God will find His instrument. I'm only the channel, not the source."

The record of the South African tour, *A Mission of Peace,* was written from newspaper reports and notes made by the Gipsy during his meetings. One wonders how he managed to find time to make the notes, or write the book which was a best-seller. The final chapter, "Retrospect," pointed out that political differences, for example, in the employment of Chinese labor in South African mines, had caused bad feeling between the people of England and those of South Africa. The Gipsy did not keep quiet when faced with a matter of principle, as in his objection to proposals that he preach to segregated audiences. He tried to bring out the best in men, even those who were mistaken.

"My purpose is to bring men together," he argued. "Not to divide them. Let them *all* come to hear the gospel."

Some would say he was politically naïve. But that was probably his strength. The book closes with a tribute to his daughter, Zillah, who did so much good work in conducting children's meetings: "She could speak to the youngest who came, for she definitely gave herself to the Lord when she was seven years old . . . oh, if we could be ten minutes ahead of the devil with every child in the land! What a world of sin and sorrow we should prevent! May God help the church to save the children!"

Yes, the work in South Africa retained a very special place in the evangelist's heart. The doors had been left wide open. Looking back upon it all, more than sixty years later, we can only ask why the churches did not remain true to his message of revival across racial barriers. But that is a question that is not to be faced by our South African brethren alone.

25

A Handful of Memories

We pause to examine the impressions of Gipsy Smith in his early twentieth century campaigns, recounted by those who saw and heard him. Of one fact there can be no doubt. He brought many people to a knowledge of Jesus Christ and his influence for good continues, all these years after the meetings were held. The impressions recorded here come from ordinary men and women in their own words.

■ A few times in my life, it was my privilege to listen to that great soul. The first occasion was at Tiverton, and two memories of that service remain with me. A fond mother, no doubt anxious to hear the Gipsy preach, brought a baby in arms to the service. Apparently the baby did not agree with all that the preacher said, and continued to cry.

Presently, the Gipsy stopped the service and said, "I know, dear woman, what that baby needs is fresh air." The hint was taken. A remark to the young people has stayed in my memory: "Young men, should you live to get on in this world and get rich enough to buy a horse and you can't get that horse to stop at the little chapel where your mother used to worship and your father used to pray, my advice to you is to sell that horse!" Also, a few years later when the Methodist Conference met at Plymouth, a sweet memory I had was taking the sacramental cup from his hand.

Mr. R. Huxtable

■ I recall that when I was a very small boy—I think about seven—Gipsy Smith's father was the preacher at a mission held in the Congregational Church at Polegate, near Eastbourne. He could not read, so his wife read the lessons.

He played the violin and accompanied the hymns. I remember him well as a very big, swarthy man, and particularly I remember that, after one of the services, he came among the congregation and put his huge hand (as it seemed to me) on my small head and said, "God bless that lad." I think that incident had more to do with the course of my life than perhaps I have hitherto realized. I am just coming up to my fiftieth year as a Methodist local preacher.

Mr. Frederick Down

■ I heard Gipsy Smith in the Methodist Central Hall, Barking Road, East Ham, about 1905. I was a member of the Ilford Gospel Choir and we occupied the stage on this special occasion. Our choirmaster and conductor was a Mr. D. J. Simons and we sang hymns, chiefly from Alexander's Hymnal. I well remember Gipsy Smith preaching to a full audience at this fine Central Hall and he did get worked up to his sermon. He did a fair amount of gesticulating, then took off his coat and carried on, and knelt down on one knee with hands clasped. Truly a wonderful inspiration to us all. . . . I well remember two of the hymns we sang at Gipsy Smith's service—"The Glory Song" (When all my labors and trials are o'er) and "Oh, It Is Wonderful" (I stand all amazed at the love Jesus offers me).

Mr. C. Thompson

■ I want to tell you of an incident that happened in a fortnight's mission by Gipsy Smith in the town of Blackburn many years ago. I was a girl of fifteen and am now eighty-three. I sang in his choir. We hired two theatres and one big hall, and I can remember the first night looking up to the top of the stage. I can see him now. There he was, standing, hat tilted, listening to our singing before the meeting started. He came down and taught us how to sing a hymn—what a lovely voice he had. He made us sing it over and over until it was perfect.

We lived next door to a very drunken family, all men. One of these was blind; his young brother had thrown a pair of scissors at him years before and blinded him. When this man, Edwin, came home drunk every night, he would pull his brother out of bed and kick him around the floor. The rows were dreadful and we youngsters were terrified. On the first night of Gipsy Smith's mission, this blind man was the first to go to the inquiry room, as we called it. My mother just could not believe it and said that it would never last. He went every night, always the first and even went (as he always did) to visit the public houses and hold a meeting. He never broke his vow of dedication, nor did he ever touch a drop of alcohol afterward. He joined the Church of England, and was successful in gradually getting his brothers to give up the drink. He held cottage meetings in his own home, and started a mission for the blind. If there was anything in the town

of a religious nature, Edwin was there, collecting for
this and that from door to door. He was a power of
good. He lived to a ripe old age, a good life, owing to
the ministry of Gipsy Smith. I shall never forget the
Gipsy saying, "A blind man shall lead them." I often
saw Edwin miles away from home—no buses then—
with bundles of leaflets under his arm, such as British
and Foreign Bible Society, giving them out, always with
a gospel message. I remember, just after his conversion, at one of his cottage meetings, his old mother
standing at the kitchen door, with a jug under her
apron to fetch her supper beer, listening to what Jesus
had done for him. I was not as ready with my pen as
I am today, or I would have written and told Gipsy
Smith about it.

                                     Mrs. M. Entwistle

When I was a small girl, I met Gipsy Smith. I am
nearly seventy now! But I have never forgotten a part
of his mission. Near my birthplace of Farnborough in
Hampshire there is a small village called Cove. My
sister and I used to go to a small corrugated iron building which was the Primitive Methodist Chapel. One
day, Gipsy Smith came to conduct a mission there.
The little place was full. Some had to come in from
the nearby alehouses; there were three only a short
distance away. Child as I was, I could see the scars
which sin and drink had made on the men from the
alehouses. I remember the Gipsy as a fine big man with
thick black hair and dark eyes which flashed as he
spoke. He talked to us children—we were in the two
front rows. I cannot remember all he said, but I clearly remember him saying, "I could have a belt made of

golden sovereigns if I wanted to, but I prefer to use my money for the Lord Jesus." Childlike, I tried to visualize how many it would take to go round his waist. He looked so big to my eyes. I missed a lot of his message—was he aware of it, I wonder? I was sitting on the first seat. He came down out of the pulpit and walked up the aisle, pausing by me. I remember that he had a lovely voice and he sang, "Sinner, how thy heart is troubled, God is coming very near, Do not hide thy deep emotion, Do not check that falling tear." We felt God was there. I saw two or three of those sin-stained people almost running into the vestry with tears streaming down their faces. I cannot remember any more, but I am happy to tell you what I know of this wonderful evangelist.

Mrs. Emily Benson

■ As a boy, I lived in the Rhondda and, when I was about eleven years of age, Gipsy Smith held a revival campaign in a huge marquee on the old fairground, now the Rhondda Transport Depot at Porth. My mother took my sister and me down to hear Gipsy Smith and, although it is more than sixty-five years since he preached at Porth, I can remember him well, a man with dark, swarthy complexion, curly black hair and eyes that seemed to bore into you. His meetings were packed to the door, and there was great enthusiasm at each meeting. If my memory is correct, one of the men converted in his campaign was a very rough character named Billy Bach (little Billy). This man joined the Salvation Army and I often saw him banging the bass drum at their open air meetings. When he died, such was his reputation as a Christian worker

that his funeral was the largest seen in the Rhondda up
till then, although the weather was atrocious. Many
people were converted at the Gipsy's meetings. One
man became a member of our little chapel at Ynyshir
and was a faithful member for over forty years.

Mr. T. Powell

■ In 1904, I took part in a mission held by Gipsy
Smith at Southend on Sea, in the large hall of the Kur-
saal, holding nearly six thousand people. It was packed
every night for nine days. My part was certainly small,
being a member of the choir of one hundred and fifty,
every night drawn from the various Free Churches in
the town. It was indeed a wonderful sight for us sitting
on the stage just behind the Gipsy and listening to his
message; watching the faces of the audience, one could
almost hear a pin drop. Certainly, we were very, very
conscious of the Spirit of God brooding over the meetings. As a result of that mission, 608 souls gave themselves to God so, for many years afterwards, the impact
of that week was felt and known.

Every night, the first two rows were reserved for
gypsies only, there being a gypsy camp at Eastwood,
then just outside the town. They came night after night
and sang with great fervor "Jesus Is Mighty to Save."
Many came out for God. One, the gypsy queen, with
her black curls on either side of her face, came to our
house one day, selling clothespins. She recognized me
and my mother, who had spoken to her at one of the
meetings, and said, "Oh, my dear, have you a piano
or organ? Do play and sing with me 'Jesus Is Mighty to
Save.'" And we did.

As a further result of that week, eight gypsy couples

went to the Avenue Baptist Church, and asked the minister (the Reverend James McCleery, now gone home) to marry them, which he did. They had been living together but now wanted to do the right thing. He married them, together in a row.

Every night of the campaign, Gipsy sang to us himself, and his voice still rings in my ears, just like a bird, so clear, every word distinct and a message. He said that he never was taught music, only by the birds, as a boy. One night he sang "Never Lose Sight of Jesus"; on another, "I Will Sing the Wondrous Story" to the Welsh tune "Hyfrydol" and, in the last line of the last verse, everybody was moved to tears, some weeping heavily.

Each night, he insisted on all doors being closed to any latecomers, and everybody quite still while the Scripture was read. He said, "Before I speak to you, let God speak and listen to Him." Doors could be kept open at all other times during the meeting. . . . His ministry was a great help to me, a young, dedicated Christian.

Miss Edith Benson

■ I was a boy of some eight or nine years when my Christian parents took me to a large meeting held in Leyton, London. He had a very lovely, strong voice which he used a lot in his meetings with emotional effect, but nevertheless he was a sincere and true soul winner. There were inquiry rooms for those who were in need of help at the close, and, in those days, buttonholing people was not frowned on. I may say I avoided passing any person who was talking to any that way, though it made an impression, so that, when I got to my home, I made the decision to get right with God. So from that time, my spiritual life grew.

Mr. A. H. Taffs

■ One of the greatest meetings of Gipsy Smith's campaign in Wales was at Bridgend Market Hall, which had been specially cleared for the occasion. I don't know how many thousands got into the hall, but the enthusiasm was overwhelming, and it is true to say that this and other tours helped to create the atmosphere and the spirit which led to the revival led by Evan Roberts, a revival which filled the churches, emptied the public houses and put crime in suspension. He told me afterward that it (the Bridgend meeting) was one of the most tremendous occasions of his life. His power was overwhelming. I recall part of his addresses:

"There are many things we do not and cannot understand. *I* cannot explain and *you* cannot explain how the power of God is manifested in the mighty cataract, how the tremendous power of God is reflected in the face of a child as it smiles in the summer sun, how the love of God is found in the cold water which brings relief to the fevered brow of a suffering soul, how He bestows joy to those who have lost all but their faith—I cannot explain these things. And I cannot tell you the precise process by which the loving Father lifts a sinner from the miriest gutter and makes a saint of him. I don't know *how* He does it, but I *know* He does it because He did it to me, Gipsy Smith."

His poetic touch was shown that night in wonderful phrases. Here is an example: "When I campaigned in Portsmouth, I had wonderful help from a dear old lady. I wish I could describe her to you. I know—she was like an old country church, lit up for divine service."

Mr. E. James

■ I was at a North London evangelistic meeting which seemed somehow very uninspiring. Suddenly, and as far as I knew, unannounced, Gipsy Smith came in and presently began to speak. Almost at once, the atmosphere changed, the meeting was alive and spiritually thrilling.

Gipsy Smith left as suddenly as he had come, and someone asked me to take him to an underground station opposite the hall. As we went, I asked Gipsy Smith why there was such a difference after he had come. "Oh, I don't know," said Gipsy Smith, "maybe it's because I have never knowingly crossed God's will."

Rev. G. B. Mountford

26

Ici On Parle Anglais

You can say no to Jesus Christ until you lose all desire to say yes.

The Gipsy's visit to France, in March, 1908, came at a time of rebellion against organized religion. For so many French people, the inquiry room and the confessional amounted to much the same thing—and they wanted none of it. However, fifty earnest Christians, working in the city of Paris, urged the evangelist to "come over and help us." They promised a good interpreter, though it would be a rare linguist indeed who could keep pace with the Gipsy's fervent appeals. They pointed to the great need of France. They persisted, so the Gipsy agreed to go and, as this was his first trip to France, took his wife with him. Such was the hostility toward religion however, that the visit had to be advertised as a conference, and the meetings held in a concert hall. The evangelist certainly felt out of place; there seemed to be no sense of consecration in the building yet, as he looked over the sea of faces that opening night, he remembered God's promise to be with him *anywhere*. Many of the audience spoke English, as circulars had been distributed among English-speaking Parisians.

As the Gipsy walked onto the stage, opera glasses

were raised. He knelt and prayed at the small table on the stage, seeking guidance and strength; then he spoke to the audience—or tried to speak, as he described the scene himself. After singing a gospel song, he spoke to the audience and told them that he was just a man who believed in the power of God to change people's lives.

"I can't claim to be any better than any of you," he said. "I often make mistakes and I often get discouraged. At such times, I ask my friends to pray for me, because I know that prayer changes things—and people."

As he spoke, very much from the heart, he found that there was a new attention from his hearers. They were touched now, not just curious onlookers.

"I wonder if you ever felt like that," he continued. "If your life isn't all that it should be, let me pray for you as tonight I pray for myself." Then he invited anyone in need of prayer simply to stand, as the Gipsy stood, and join him in a simple prayer. To his joy and amazement, some two thirds of the audience rose to their feet.

There was no inquiry room, so the Gipsy just committed the people to God's keeping power. After a few of these meetings, he designed a simple decision card. The wording was simple enough: "Believing Jesus Christ to be the only Saviour for sinners, I do here and now accept Him as my Lord and Saviour, and promise by His grace to love and follow Him." There was room for a signature and a church connection, if any. The cards were left behind so that the organizers of the conference could follow up inquirers. On the very first night when the cards were used, about one hundred and fifty were signed. It was not long before the audience was largely made up of people who spoke only their native tongue, French, and the interpreter had to be brought in. We can only sympathize with the poor man, who did his best, but who was quite unable to convey the Gipsy's sentiments to the audience. It was, for the Gipsy himself, a time of utter agony. Finally, the evangelist thanked the interpreter and said that he would carry on alone. He knew a little Fench, and asked that simple but forthright question: "Do you love Jesus?" At once, people all over the auditorium jumped to their feet and responded *"Oui, oui!"*

One could say that it was the Gipsy's shortest sermon ever. He knew too little French to say much more—and wept that he could not. But it was enough.

Widespread public apathy about matters of religion certainly saddened the evangelist. "Where men deny God, it isn't long before they invite the devil," he said.

A year later he returned to Paris, and was invited to a very unusual house meeting held at the home of a very wealthy woman. She was in fact a young Christian, having been converted at the Paris conference a year before. Twenty-five protestant pastors had been invited to lunch, she explained, and this would give the Gipsy an opportunity to talk to them. At first, he was reluctant. In 1908, he had found so many of these pastors inclined to Unitarianism or rationalistic views. However, he went, and it proved to be a time of revival. For more than two hours, he answered questions through an interpreter. The ministerial lunch was such a success that it was followed by another, and this time more than seventy pastors came.

"I'm sure that they returned to their church fortified

in faith and the desire to evangelize," the Gipsy remarked. Had he been able to speak French, and had his heavy schedule permitted, he could have spoken from many French pulpits after that!

The Gipsy went to France again, but this time in khaki. He was fifty-four when the war was declared on August 4, 1914, looking more than ever like "a prosperous timber merchant" (it may be recalled that he used to sell clothespins). The old fire remained, but his style had mellowed and, in a way, made him more effective. He must have seemed a father figure to many of the young soldiers whom he met on the battlefield. It would have been easy enough for him to stay by his fireside at Romany Tan, and to let the thunder of war roll ignored, like a distant storm. As it was, he decided that his place was at the front. The authorities, he explained, found out about his disability when he had wanted to join up—he was born too long ago! But he went to France under the auspices of the YMCA, as a g e n e r a l evangelist-cum-postman-cum-dispenser of chocolate, soap, stationery and other useful items. He did what he could. It was not much, perhaps. As no few chaplains discovered, the horror of that war made a crucifixion not only of man but of his hopes. It was a testing time for any man's faith, the preacher's more than most. Naturally, the Gipsy followed the approach of that other saint in the battlefield, Studdert Kennedy. He went out to be one of them, not just as a passing minister eager to return to quieter scenes. Gipsy, for example, was not too impressed with the "red hot gospeller" who tried to interrupt a woman's serving of refreshments to weary soldiers in order to give them a dose of the gospel.

"You don't have to tell us about Jesus, guv'nor," a young soldier piped up. "She puts it into the coffee."

His approach was tailor-made to the situation. In the first place, he was a remarkably interesting speaker. Critics never paused to consider what kind of fortune he could have had as an entertainer. And he always met the soldiers on their own terms. Some of the officers seemed baffled by it all, like the colonel who announced that "Gipsy Smith will now . . . er . . . entertain. . . ."

When he sang with the troops, he did not rush in with some religious song or hymn. Around some battered piano, in some crowded hut or canteen, the Gipsy would lead in those songs which were so much part of World War I. Then, when he felt that the time was suitable, he would suggest that they sing one for the folks at home—that usually turned out to be a well-known hymn chosen by one of the men. It was not hard to say a short prayer after that. Sometimes, the Gipsy would go on to talk about his father's conversion, or give his own testimony. He possessed a quite remarkable perception of what would be appropriate for that particular audience. Many young soldiers stood when the Gipsy invited them to commit their lives to Christ.

"Boys," he would tell them. "None of us have much to hang on to in this world. But if you have given your heart to Jesus, He'll hang on to you. He has the power to save—and to keep, wherever you are. Always remember that!"

Sentimental? The Gipsy often met men who were converted during that front-line ministry, many during his second visit to Australia in 1926. "Front-line preaching is a test of any man's preaching and his religion," he said. "It makes you realize how essential the essentials are, and how important it is to preach them."

Yes, and it would have done many ministers good to visit France and meet the boys to whom the church—up to now—had meant little, if anything. Just as he had been ill at ease in that sophisticated concert hall in 1908, now the Gipsy was thoroughly at home. He could be of evident service to those men who had gone out for king and country. Once, he was due to speak to a regiment, largely made up of Irish Roman Catholics. He advertised his subject as Gypsy Life—on which he was certainly an authority. The hut was crowded. About eight hundred soldiers turned up to hear a lively talk about the history of the gypsies and some of the tricks of their trade. When he had been talking for about half an hour, he stopped and suggested that they continue the story on the following evening. For six successive nights, the Gipsy kept the men enthralled. He did not talk about religion, or say anything that might cut across their own religious loyalties. But he talked about nature, his childhood, his life—and Jesus. One of the soldiers grasped the Gipsy's hand.

"Your Riverince, ye're a gintleman!"

He kept his eye on that young soldier and, a little later, told him about the song that God had put into his heart. The soldier wistfully said that he would like that song, but that the Gipsy would ask him to give up his religion.

"Not at all," the Gipsy replied. "It's not your religion you have to give up—it's your sin!"

So the young soldier was converted.

The toughest job was saying goodbye to the soldiers as they went up to the trenches. Sometimes the Gipsy could hardly hear himself speak above the gunfire and the crackle of machine guns. Just as Studdert Kennedy in another place found his young soldiers ready to cheer for Christ, so the Gipsy found many wanting to call upon the name of the Lord. He spent as much time as he could in France.

"Whenever I'm back in England, I think of the boys," he explained. "And I always want to be back there with them!"

Someone called him a giver out of good things. He did give out letters, chocolate, buttons, and many other things as we have seen. It always gave him great joy to be able to tell anxious parents at home that he had met their son at the front and that he was well and still serving Jesus. Collections in aid of items for the troops, stationery, for example, were taken at the Gipsy's meetings in England. He always carried a liberal supply when he went to France.

"If a soldier asks me for one sheet of paper, I know he's writing to his mother," he said. "But if he wants two, he's writing to the girl friend!"

There were times of great sadness too, for the Gipsy often had occasion to talk to men whose time on earth was fast running out. He carried last messages to mothers back home and always insured that they were delivered.

Once, he visited a hospital for the limbless, and was amazed at the great cheerfulness of the patients. One, who had lost both arms and both legs, told the Gipsy he would surely save a lot of money on tailor's bills.

"Aren't men *worth* saving?" the Gipsy cried. "This war has shown us so much brutality. But it has shown me so much bravery, so much love men have for one another. . . . Shouldn't we be eager to save every one?"

Many will still remember him, a middle-aged, stocky man in khaki, somehow looking a little out of place, pouring out the tea and coffee in some canteen, and cheering cold and weary men that were often so young. It was one of the greatest ministries the Gipsy ever performed.

He was honored as a Member of the British Empire for his war service. The title, in practice, meant little, but it was an honor he was glad to accept. Few British evangelists have been so decorated. On several occasions he attended garden parties at Buckingham Palace, and Queen Mary was keenly interested in the Gipsy's work.

"Perhaps I'll get a title one day," he said. "Lord Clothespins!"

27

The Golden Years of Gipsy Smith

What does God think of us, those of us who are professing Christians? He sees not what we appear, but what we are.

In the early 1920's, the Gipsy discovered a song which had a profound influence upon his ministry. Written by Leonard Voke, it was called "Can Others See Jesus in You?" The first chorus turned the question inward, "May others see Jesus in me?" but the remaining two finished with the phrase:

> For how will the lost know of Jesus
> If they fail to see Jesus in you?

It is the question we have to keep asking. Certainly, it was one of the Gipsy's favorite solos and it was recorded by Columbia Records. The evangelist was now in his sixties, but chuckled whenever anyone said anything about retirement.

"The good Lord hasn't told me anything about *that*," he would retort.

The Methodist church became his "spiritual home of adoption," though he was always ready to preach anywhere. He joined the Hills Road Methodist Church in Cambridge and thought it a real luxury to sit down and hear someone else preach. Although he remained an evangelistic preacher to the end of his days, the nineteen-twenties saw Gipsy aware of the need of holiness, of godly living, in the church. He had seen so much revival, and declared that it began only when some Christians got down to the task of living out the gospel. That handsome, burly and beaming man would urge his congregation to look as though they rejoiced.

"My word!" he used to say. "If some of you live like you look, the Lord help those you live with! The criterion for Christian living is simple enough—it is Jesus Himself."

He would go on to talk of the beauty of Jesus which was to make His followers beautiful too. "Yet," he would sigh, "we often look about as beautiful as some poor old tramp."

It is strange some of his critics said that all he thought about was money for the Gipsy used to say, loud and clear, "what really counts is service and sacrifice, love for others and a constant passion to follow Jesus whole-heartedly." Compared to that, "giving money is no more than a good habit, and it is certainly not the kind of exciting Christianty I want to see in the church."

The whole tone of his ministry can be seen in something he said during this period. "Without the Holy Spirit, we may as well close down our churches and keep our Bibles closed. You might as well attempt to make a hole in a concrete wall with a candle, as to get converts without the Holy Spirit."

This was not essentially new, of course. He had always been a man much given to prayer, and had seen

the amazing revival in South Africa in 1904. But the
1920's with its escapism and apparent forgetfulness of
all the sacrifice of the war surely saddened him. He
must have realized that the pressing need was for a
revived Church shining as a light in an evil world. And
that, he was sure, could only come when Christians
started following Jesus in earnest. So the Gipsy's sixtieth birthday, in 1920, marked something of a water-
shed in the course of his life. The firebrand had turned
into a steady, bright flame at which men could warm
their hands and their hearts. He still preached his
evangelical sermons, like "The Lost Christ," but his
mind seemed to be turning more and more to preparation for the life beyond this.

One day, in Bishop Auckland, a town in northeast
England, he decided to use a little verse that he had
heard at Cliff College of Evangelism. This was the
well-known song, "Let the Beauty of Jesus Be Seen in
Me." It was a memorable if simple piece and became,
first, the theme song of the Bishop Auckland campaign,
and, eventually, the Gipsy's signature tune. He used the
title *The Beauty of Jesus* for a book which he wrote in
the early 1930's. His voice, even at that age, was still
strong.

"I'm just like the birds," he explained. "I get plenty
of practice." This was true. At virtually all the campaigns he conducted, he sang. The collections of solos
sung by Gipsy Smith were bestsellers in their day; the
songs themselves retained their popularity. One of the
most successful was "Not Dreaming," written by Gipsy
Smith and his American accompanist, Edwin Young. It
seemed that the Gipsy was quietly sitting in the corner
of a railway compartment, reflecting on all the wonder-

ful events of a recent campaign. As he was tired, he had his eyes closed, but he was not asleep. A couple of teenagers entered the compartment and one said, "Oh, he's only dreaming!" before going on their way. A song came into the Gipsy's mind: "If I am dreaming, let me dream on." Edwin Young put music to the words, and so the Gipsy had another one for his repertoire, as did countless gospel singers all over the world.

Railroad travel in the USA did not perturb the Gipsy at all—indeed, it had much in common with the well-furnished gypsy wagon travel of his childhood, though, as he pointed out, the railroad companies had faster timetables. As the above anecdote shows, he acquired some good material for his talks and songs while traveling by rail and he also made plenty of friends. It was quite characteristic of the Gipsy to inquire of the porter or dining car attendant, "Do you love Jesus?" and nothing gave him greater pleasure than the beamed reply, "I sure do, Mr. Smith."

Although aggression was not in the Gipsy's gentle nature, he was ready to counter the modernist outlook of travelers who wanted to find out more of the Gipsy's brand of religion. One suggested that man's troubles were due to his environment.

"No one had a better environment than Adam," responded the Gipsy. "And that didn't stop him from sinning."

Some of the Gipsy's traveling schedules looked like a whistle-stop tour which probably explains the tremendous number of friends he had throughout the USA—including Billy Sunday, Dr. DeWitt Talmage,

Dr. Henry Ward Beecher, and countless writers, news-
papermen, small town pastors and preachers, and women workers in downtown churches. As someone once
remarked, "He's been everywhere and met everyone."
Walking with the great made no difference to the Gipsy,
or indeed to his preaching style. However, he did gain
a tremendous arsenal of stories and memories for his
talks, given, when necessary, off-the-cuff. In the opinion of the Reverend James Vance, Chairman of the
Nashville Campaign Executive Committee, Gipsy's
off-the-cuff addresses, given at noonday meetings at
Nashville, in the spring of 1922, achieved great heights
of pulpit power. The Ryman Auditorium, used for the
noonday and evening meetings of the Nashville Campaign, proved to be far too small for all who wished
to enter.

Every day for the noon meeting, a local pastor was
teamed with the evangelist and, for the first ten
minutes, the local man spoke on a passage of scripture
chosen by himself. Then, without any preparation or
foreknowledge of the scripture to be expounded, the
Gipsy took up the theme in an impromptu address. He
never once failed to link his words with what had gone
before—a quite remarkable achievement for one whose
theological training had been among the trees! The un-
scripted talks, taken down by a stenographer, were
subsequently published in the USA and in England.

He was still covering a lot of ground—and sea! In
1926, he went back to Australia where he was to meet
plenty of old friends, as well as people who had been
converted during his first Australian mission long before. Three of the ministers working with the Gipsy at
Adelaide were men who had been converted through

his ministry, and the evangelist met many who recalled his words to them when they were serving in France, during the war. Sydney, Melbourne, and countless small towns heard the evangelist. This time, the Gipsy used radio to swell his congregation—an innovation that did not, in any way, diminish the power of the message. Here, as in the Billy Graham television relays of our time, the transmission seemed to make no difference in the sense of presence of a prophet.

His twenty-fifth trip to the USA was made in 1928, an especially happy occasion when, with his evangelist son, Albany (sometimes known as "Gipsy Smith, Jr."), he conducted meetings at Mexia and Waco, in Texas. Albany had decided to become a full-time evangelist some five years earlier, and was relatively well-known in the southern states. A resident of Noank, Connecticut, Albany had something of the winsome approach of his father and conducted many great campaigns.

Gipsy himself went to Mexia on the invitation of a minister, the local Rotary Club and the Chamber of Commerce, who together arranged the building of a church to house the campaign. The evangelist was very much impressed by this practical expression of their faith—the Americans, he later told his English audiences, are very fast to act on the promise of great things.

The 1928 schedule took in Greenville, Ohio; Battle Creek, Michigan; Nashville; Chicago; Los Angeles and Long Beach, where Gipsy preached in a tent to over five thousand people. One of his old friends, the celebrated preacher, Dr. G. Campbell Morgan, came along to help Gipsy in the Los Angeles campaign, though help is perhaps not the right word. They were old friends who loved the work of evangelism. At sixty-eight years of age, the Gipsy was as lively as ever, able to touch his toes twenty times in succession—an exercise he recommended to preachers who wanted to keep in trim. Dr. Campbell Morgan, well-known in the USA for his preaching and written works, used the occasion to thank God for friendship and encouragement in their respective ministries.

Gipsy also visited Toronto, after an absence of some nineteen years, meeting some ministers who had been converted at the Gipsy's campaigns in England.

Yet, despite the wonderful blessings enjoyed in the campaigns of the period, there were still those who declared that the days of evangelistic campaigns were over. It was a question that often came up at the Gipsy's press interviews.

"I hardly know what to say when I'm faced with that one," he would tell the reporters. "At the recent campaign at Nashville, for instance, I saw that the strength of many churches came from converts of the campaign we conducted about six years ago."

And if any reporter inquired what the Gipsy was going to do next in the way of reviving the churches, the evangelist would say, gently but firmly, that the initiative was, first, with the Lord (who alone could revive anything or anyone), and, second, with the ministers and members of local churches. Gipsy never saw himself as a loner. He would work with churches, or not at all, as far as campaigns were concerned.

In that memorable campaign at Nashville, by the way, the Gipsy spoke to a house meeting of some three hundred and fifty people, arranged by one of the campaign converts, a lady of some social standing in the town. At the end of the 1928 tour, he felt, more than ever, that people were hungry for simple but thought-provoking, direct, objective preaching. Not emotional parties which, in the long run, would do little for the church, he emphasized, but truthful, sincere declarations of the gospel. Although (like evangelists in our own day) he was accused of creating emotionalism, he was, in fact, far less emotional than many of his pulpit contemporaries. He was a poet with words that touched the heart. In one of his American addresses, he recalled a return visit to the English country lane in which his mother had died. The lane was much as it had been all those years before, and Gipsy took a root from the grassy bank, to plant at his home at Cambridge.

"I planted it beneath a pear tree, where I knew it would be sheltered from the cold winter winds, and where it would catch the first kiss of the spring sunshine. One day, when I was touring in America, I had a letter from my wife, in which she told me that the old root had produced a beautiful bank of primroses. My friends, your life is like that. You don't know what's inside of you until you let God's sunshine bring it out. Give God a chance to bring out the beauty in your life."

That was the Gipsy's essential message. A book of memories produced in Britain in the early 1930s was called *The Beauty of Jesus*. It summed up his style of evangelism in the USA as everywhere else. That he was a walking advertisement for his message can be seen from the comment of a well-meaning American lady who told the Gipsy that she had heard his father some thirty years earlier, and that he had looked much as Gipsy did now. The Gipsy smiled, for as his father had never visited America, she was referring to him— as he had been those decades earlier.

Arriving home in England in May, Gipsy was already planning the next American tour. Strange as it must seem, he was in greater demand in the USA than in his own country and had sufficient invitations to fill every week in his diary for the next five years. His principle of going only to towns where ministers and churches were united in their decision to conduct a campaign was one reason why invitations for British campaigns were sparse. The decline of interest in campaign evangelism in Britain sprang from this period.

The Gipsy spent seven months in Australia, and the conversion rate was more than eleven thousand a month. In all, some eighty thousand decision cards were signed during the series of meetings, which embraced Tasmania as well as the Australian mainland.

In 1929, as the world approached the brink of financial insanity, the Gipsy went to America. Ocean Grove gave him a wonderful welcome, and the Gipsy went on to preach at Germantown, Pennsylvania; Rochester and Indianapolis, Indiana; North Carolina; and Texas (as well as a few other places in between). The stay at Indianapolis was supposed to be a rest. Some rest! On Thursday evening, he talked to a large audience at the Methodist Episcopal Church at nearby Rochester, Indiana, and on the following Sunday morning, spoke to a welcoming congregation at the Central Avenue Methodist Episcopal Church in Indianapolis. Some of the good folk had gone into the church at 8:30 A.M. in order to obtain a seat for the 10:45 A.M. meeting. The Gipsy had held a campaign at the church thirty-six years before (as well as another in 1921), so he was able to meet many converts whose faith had weathered the years. What amazing stamina he possessed. Away from his home in England for nine months, he had only two Sundays free during that time, and went as far west as Los Angeles and as far south as Atlanta, Georgia. He was never late for a meeting, nor did he miss one. Not at all a bad record for a man only months away from his seventieth birthday!

In America, as in South Africa in 1904, he encountered the racial problem. The Gipsy never felt ill at ease with black people; on the contrary, he found them good company. "I wish I could take singing like that back home with me," he told one group of highly vocal black workers.

Prophetically, the Gipsy wrote that only Christianity could deal with the problem of the color line. He added that it was also the only thing that can save the world from revolution.

Looking like "a father in Christ," as well as speaking like one, the Gipsy said of the American tour, "I've found a new theme or, rather, I've learned to re-emphasize the old one of personal consecration." He broadcast over the radio in America, too (on one occasion to an audience of fifteen million) and the Gipsy learned of some people who had been touched by this relatively new medium. Had there been time, the Gipsy could have made very many broadcasts while in America.

"Some people thump the tub," he explained. "I try to touch the heart."

He was self-effacing, too. Over the years, he had

welcomed publicity as a means of bringing people to the meetings, though he had certainly suffered from the over-exuberance of reporters. Now, at sixty-nine, he was just a little weary of journalistic exaggeration. One paper called him "traveling man for the King of kings, optimist, patriot and lover of mankind" and another announced, in the largest type available, "Prepare for a big shock! Gipsy Smith, the little minister, is coming!"

The reporters were often surprised when the Gipsy told them he held no doctor's degree, for most preachers of note held doctorates! "My health is sound and my preaching is sound," he pointed out. "So why should I want to be a doctor?"

The press seemed similarly astonished when they discovered the Gipsy came very much on his own, apart from members of the family, and his accompanist. Reporters seemed to think that the Gipsy should have an organization.

"My Master organizes the universe, if that is good enough!" The Gipsy would make some comment of that kind, and then say a few words to the reporters as sinners in need of a Saviour. They were never hostile to the evangelist, but more than one one went away, shaking his head in amazement: "What does that guy think he can do on his own?"

The campaigns were the source of great encouragement and renewal for the churches. In San Antonio alone, more than 10,000 decision cards were signed; in Winston-Salem, North Carolina, nearly three times that number (27,500) were returned. And now, more than ever, the Gipsy's preaching was tempered by a sober, restrained appeal. He knew, better perhaps than the people who came forward, how hard it would be for them to go all the way with Jesus.

The world went mad in 1929. It was the beginning of the great depression, the end of the jazz age which the evangelist so much deplored. When he recalled the thousands of conversions during the 1929 campaigns in America, the Gipsy felt sure that God was ready to save to the uttermost those who might soon lose everything else. It was certainly the message he took across the Atlantic when he returned to America in 1932.

28

Full Circle

*Some folks are religious tramps, all the religion they
have is in the heels of their boots, going to meetings.*

"We were expecting someone older," the steward
said, surprised as the Gipsy strode into the vestry. Even
at seventy, the evangelist looked like a middle-aged
businessman, bright and full of optimism. He was, in
1931, the elder statesman of Methodism or, to be
more accurate, the elder statesman of evangelism,
traveling, speaking and writing.

The house at Cambridge was "open house" for visitors, though the Gipsy often preferred to be alone
with his friends and family, and to have time in which
he could prepare for his many engagements. It was a
busy household, but well-staffed by people who had
remained under his roof for many years. For example,
the Gipsy, in 1931, expressed his gratitude to his wife's
companion, Elizabeth Parkes, who had held the post
for forty-three years. The maid, Bertha, had been in
the household for twenty-four years, and the gardener,
Mr. Pearson, for twenty-two. Romany Tan was a happy home—no artificial air of piety prevailed here, but
warm and godly cheerfulness. As the Gipsy remarked,
"the best test of a man's character is his home." One
of the better-known members of the household was
Will Sizer, chauffeur and lay preacher.

"If ever the car breaks down and he can't start it again—a very unlikely event—I know that Will can run ahead and give the folk a good sermon."

The car, presented to the Gipsy by American friends, was roomy, comfortable and fast. It certainly covered a lot of ground. The Gipsy liked to go on preaching tours with one or two friends, taking in as many churches as possible, including a few in secluded places. In 1931, for example, Reverend Dr. F. Luke Wiseman accompanied the evangelist in a lightning tour between Wellingborough in Northamptonshire and Beverley in Yorkshire. The Gipsy called these the "good companions" tours.

"The scenery didn't move so fast in the old days when I lived in a gypsy wagon!" On one famous occasion, two friends traveling with the Gipsy left the car to walk up a steep hill to have a good view. They left the evangelist in the car, thinking that the walk would be too strenuous for a man in his seventies. But he had the last laugh. Always observant, he had been watching the wild birds and pointed out a couple of nests which his colleagues had not noticed. He was certainly a keen student of nature: like his nephew, Romany, he could have written some marvelous books on the subject, if he had had the time!

One nature scene few people will forget is the Dutch Barn at Skillington, a small village near Grantham in Lincolnshire. The normal population of four hundred temporarily increased four-fold one day in 1932, when the Gipsy came to conduct a meeting arranged by the Grantham Methodist Circuit. It was a very large building, a sort of cathedral with a corrugated iron roof. An entire haystack had been moved for the occasion—

though not all the chickens, according to Harold Murray, the Gipsy's beloved pianist and biographer. In addition to Harold Murray and the Gipsy, the "good companions" at Skillington included the Reverend J. A. Broadbelt, the Reverend C. H. Hulbert, the Reverend A. S. Hullah, the Reverend J. Day, and the ever-ready Will Sizer.

A handsome piano stood on a platform made of planks and a crowd of some fifteen hundred people stood under the barn roof. More stood outside. The Gipsy had some trouble with the microphone and placed his felt hat over it. He had no need of it. The Gipsy sang "Lean on His Arms, Trusting in His Love" and made his usual appeal. Many people, including some young men at the rear of the crowd, stood as a mark of their commitment to Christ. Two local vicars sat on the platform; one of them, a man of prayer and in sympathy with the Gipsy, announced that tea was available at Skillington parsonage for anyone who wanted it.

The Gipsy thought that some two thousand might turn up for supper. Certainly, everyone was fed that day, a miracle of giving and organization. Years later, people recalled the great day in Skillington barn, and the challenge that Gipsy gave to the Christians present: "In the name of God, I ask you if you have done anything specifically to bring Jesus Christ to the people? You may get very fussy and excited over an entertainment, festival, social, bazaar, circuit gathering. Do you ever get tired out in trying to secure conversions?"

This uncompromising approach did much to encourage the young 'graduates' of the Cliff College of Evangelism. Gipsy, like many of his young evangelist friends, was influenced by the example of principal, Samuel ('Sam') Chadwick, who was surely one of the spiritual giants of the century. The Cliff College Anniversary of 1932 was the last in which Gipsy and Principal Chadwick shared the same platform, for Sam Chadwick died soon afterwards. "The trouble with most of us," Sam Chadwick said, "is that our religion is too commonplace, too paltry in view of the promise that every believing heart may be filled with all the fullness of God. The supreme test of the spiritual life of every generation is its recognition and experience of the Holy Spirit, and there are thousands among us who have not so much as heard that the Spirit is given. . . . An unlearned man with the Spirit is mightier than a host of academics without Him."

Gipsy followed up the principal's words with the solo, "Jesus Revealed in Me."

His involvement with the work at Cliff College marked an important turning point in the Gipsy's life. As a sort of headquarters for the encouragement of evangelism in Britain, Cliff College attracted great numbers of people for its public meetings and anniversaries (as it still does). Thus, Gipsy found that he was receiving more and more invitations to conduct campaigns at churches in Britain, and was happy to share the platform with young firebrands from Cliff College (like Herbert Silverwood, the "Yorkshire Firebrand," as he was called) as well as with prominent evangelists and writers of the period, including, for example, Dr. F. Luke Wiseman and Hugh Redwood of the London *News Chronicle*. His campaigns were now organized by the Methodist Home Missions Department, so that the Gipsy was not a freelance, but an evangelist with official Methodist backing. Nor was he alone now, but part of a group which he happily called "the good companions."

"The good companions"—Gipsy and the Reverends Hulbert and Broadbelt, and Mr. Harold Murray—traveled all over Britain in the 1930s. The Gipsy seemed to prefer this team ministry approach, though he was just as forthright in his own views.

"The greatest barrier between your unconverted friends and Jesus is your inconsistency," he told his congregation at Jersey in 1934.

Some of his phrases gained a currency of their own, for example, "Who put your name on the church roll? Unless the Lord put it there, it ought to come off. It was the Lord who added to the church daily, and only He has any right to do it now."

It is not likely that he would change his style or the context of his message, were he alive today. Considering he was a grand old man, his voice remained remarkably strong, although recordings suggest his singing was a little strained in the higher registers. He did not miss any opportunity for an open air meeting, and invariably held his audience even with the inevitable distractions of traffic and passersby. Choosing a text, he would give a short, impromptu address, repeating the text so that it would be remembered. The forecourt of Wesley's Chapel in City Road, London, would be filled almost to capacity on such occasions. Open air meetings at the Cliff College of Evangelism were probably his favorites. It was very much in his blood and, as he said, "Jesus did much of *His* preaching in the open air, so I am just following a good example."

The most moving open air meeting conducted by the

Gipsy was, perhaps, that held in 1934 near to the very spot where Polly Smith, his mother, died. A stage was erected in the dell, a natural amphitheatre and, during the course of an address heard by three to four thousand people, the evangelist pointed to the place where, all those years before, his sister had told him, "Rodney, you have no mother!"

It was about this time that the Letchworth Methodist Circuit, consisting of just two churches, decided new premises were needed at Norton Village. Mr. Charles Cooper, secretary of the church, thought it would be appropriate to dedicate new buildings to the memory of Gipsy Smith's parents, a suggestion as warmly received by the members as by the evangelist himself. Indeed, he was responsible for raising a large sum of money for the building, gifts being donated from friends on both sides of the Atlantic.

Opened in 1934 as Norton Methodist Mission, the building (now North Avenue Methodist Church, Letchworth Garden City), has a pulpit shaped like a gypsy wagon. An inscription reads: "to the Glory of God and in memory of the beloved parents of Gipsy Smith." It was a source of great satisfaction to the evangelist, knowing that his parents' graves were such a short distance away from the pulpit, from which the gospel would be preached. It was, as he said, a lovely thought and a lovely church.

The Gipsy was in America when the campaign was opened by his daughter, Zillah, and her husband, Mr. J. T. Lean. Later, however, he and his brother, Ezekiel, conducted evangelical meetings at the church, one of the very rare occasions when the two brothers appeared on the same platform.

29

More Memories

■ I have been a member of the West London Mission ever since I came to London, very many years ago. In the early 1920s I was learning to write shorthand, and my teacher said the best way to get up a speed was to take down the sermon on Sundays. In 1923, Gipsy came to Kingsway Hall to conduct a Mission—I think it was for ten days. The place was packed each night, the people sat on every stair, and some were left standing down the sides of the hall. On one Sunday evening we had an overflow meeting in either the Aldwych or Strand Theatre—I cannot remember which—and this the Rev. Ernest Rattenbury conducted.

The services certainly were memorable and I did what the teacher suggested and took my notebook with me all the while. The Gipsy spoke to me the day that he preached on "The Lost Christ." I told him I was a member of Kingsway and was learning shorthand. He asked me to let him have a copy of my transcript, which I did. I didn't get any further comments on it, so presumed it was passable.

There was an elderly man sitting right in the front row of the hall. He had white hair and a very happy face. After leaving the hall he spoke to me. He said he had come down from the north of England and was very deaf so could not hear what the Gipsy said, but had felt the wonderful effect of the service. Would I let him have a copy of the sermon, and this I did. It transpired he was a Methodist class leader and he read the sermon to his people and spoke of the wonderful effect that the Gipsy had on him. He sent me a donation, which was the first that I had ever received for the work of the Mission.

Miss Muriel Place

■ I live at Long Sutton, which is thirteen miles from Spalding, and I am a Baptist deacon. I have often mentioned to others about the time when I journeyed to the Crescent Methodist Church, which is now demolished. I believe it held a thousand people who came to hear him. I can see him now: he came into the pulpit and went down on his knees with his arms on the top rail, which was to me very moving. He preached a powerful sermon on the cross and saving grace. He had a quality of voice that was so appealing and moving. The chapel was packed and, at the end, I felt I wanted to rise and shake hands with everyone present.

Mr. Walter Freeman

■ I am eternally grateful to this messenger of God. On a Sunday evening in 1933, my fiancé and I heard him speak in a BBC service, and his message on John 3:16 brought spiritual stirrings that led to my loved one's conversion soon after. I had been praying for this, knowing that I could never face an "unequal yoke," so my joy was two-fold. A radiant Christian, my husband gave his life early in the war (1940) and the knowledge that he is with the Lord, together with the wonderful grace of God, has enabled me to keep going on until we see Him face to face. Just one testimony I am sure to Gipsy Smith's gift of communicating the gospel by the power of the Holy Spirit and with simplicity.

Mrs. Winifred Hibbins

■ I cannot claim to have known him personally. But, when I was in my teens and early twenties, I heard the Gipsy preach and sing often and always with spiritual blessing. He was a powerful speaker. He had great gifts of imagination and heart. He was, with all his faults, completely given to Christ and dedicated to the work of evangelism to which he was called and commissioned. He was an individualist who conformed to no school of thought.

Among some ministers he was regarded with less than enthusiasm perhaps for this reason. His preaching was at times rather overcharged with emotion, but it seemed to me to arise naturally from a nature that felt strongly and could not be dispassionate and cool on matters that burned like a fire in his soul. So the emotion was Gipsy Smith being himself, but himself fired by the Holy Spirit and his passion for souls. At times, he could be hard-hitting and trenchant, as on the occasion when he held a midday service here at Grantham in the Finkin Street Methodist Church. Getting to grips with the matter of prayer and prayerlessness, I can recall as if it was yesterday how he made his congregation squirm as he banged the pulpit and said "You call yourself a Christian and never pray! What a humbug you are! What a hypocrite! What a walking fraud!" And they would take it from Gipsy, right from the shoulder.

I can recall another occasion. It was the Cliff College Anniversary in 1936. I had been a student there from 1934 to 1935 and Mr. Broadbelt, who was a friend of the Gipsy's, invited me for the weekend as a guest. I had tea with the Gipsy. In the evening he preached with great power to the crowd on the lawn. I can remember how he held them as he cried, with tears running down his cheeks, "Don't you dare to thwart the Holy Spirit! If He is calling you, don't stand in His way!"

Mr. Gordon Wyllie

■ My wife and I entertained Gipsy Smith when, in 1936 he came to conduct a mission at Oxford Place Chapel, Leeds. The idea came from the Rev. Dr. F. Luke Wiseman. At that time, Oxford Place Chapel was full every Sunday—so was Brunswick Chapel, with Dr. Leslie D. Weatherhead as the minister.

I met Gipsy Smith at the Central Station, Leeds. In five minutes, he was talking with the porter who was carrying his bag, inviting him to the special service that night.

He was an ideal guest and had a wonderful influence in the home, especially over our maid. She thought he was "super"! Others will refer to his evangelism, but I speak about him as a welcome guest in the home. He held us spellbound as he talked about the birds of the forest and beauties of woodland, and the little animals of the forest.

Before going to sleep he usually read *The Three Musketeers,* and delighted to talk about his reading.

Each night of the five-day mission the church was packed. The stewards estimated about three thousand people came each night to hear him sing and speak. They traveled from all parts of the West Riding of

Yorkshire. His messages were most challenging. His searching sermons were shot through with reason and emotion, and hundreds of people registered the intention to dedicate their lives to Christ and the work of His church. All kinds of people attended these meetings: college professors, students from Headingly College and Leeds University, business men and young people sat side by side.

After an exhausting evening, he would return to our home and immediately sit on a stool with his back to the fire. I asked him why he did this. "Always after a a meeting when I am hot I find this habit an excellent thing to do," he said. "It prevents me getting a cold or any rheumatic pains."

All over the world there are people who have been influenced for good by the ministry and memory of Gipsy Smith. My wife and I count it a high privilege to have had the opportunity of acting as host when he came to Leeds.

Rev. J. T. Hodgson, M.B.E., T.D.

■ I remember hearing him address the students at Cliff College as long ago as 1930; and he said that, as a boy, he used to watch the clouds chasing one another like ivory chariots across the canopy of heaven. He also referred to how he used to go into the fields and watch rabbits at play.

I recall a particularly outstanding talk he gave to us students on the subject of soul winning. He concluded by saying that he sometimes wrestled with God in prayer, especially when he thought he was not getting as many souls for God as he should have been. He would say, "Lord, if you don't give me more souls, I shall die!" and ended his talk with the question "Have you ever prayed like that?"

At Southport, Gipsy conducted a special service for the high school and Girl Guides. When he came to make his appeal for converts, he said with tears in his eyes, "Oh, you beautiful young women, all in the prime of life, what can I do for you? I would lay myself prostrate on the floor of this church all through the night to see you converted." How they responded! They lined up to reach the Communion rail!

Rev. C. Johns

■ During one of the meetings (at Watford in 1934) the Gipsy was holding the audience spellbound so that one could have heard a pin drop. Suddenly, there was a disturbance in a corner and he begged everyone to be quiet and not to disturb the atmosphere. Unfortunately, one of the water pipes had developed a leak and those nearby were being soaked and were not able to move! At another meeting, he was talking about the value of prayer and prayer meetings. He turned to the minister and asked him on which day of the week the church prayer meeting was held. Quickly, the minister replied, "There is a special one tomorrow night, Gipsy!" Of course, there had not been any prayer meeting planned at the church!

Mrs. Kathleen Spence

■ For twenty years (July 1933 to June 1953) I was the organist of the Hull Queen's Hall, now demolished, but in those days the headquarters of the Hull Mission Circuit. I well remember Gipsy Smith coming to the hall but cannot be sure even of the year now: I estimate that it could have been either 1935 or 1936. A rather stocky man, swarthy of appearance, with a full moustache, he preached for the conversion of souls and his audience approach was emotional. Looking rather like a prosperous businessman, energetic and full of vitality, he quipped about the fact that he used to be in the timber trade—selling clothespins!

At this particular meeting he stumbled up the platform stairs (the canvas being extremely worn in places), thus causing the trustees to carry out necessary repairs within the week. After the meeting had got under way, he pulled my jacket (he was seated just below the organ console), and asked me would I play for him when he sang. Of course I agreed—how could I do otherwise? and in front of two thousand people he rubbed both my cheeks vigorously between his hands and whispered, "Mind you play in tune, boy. It's for *Him!*" Gipsy Smith's singing voice was in the tenor range, powerful and clear in tone, albeit the appeal again was to the emotions. On this occasion I recollect he sang "Wonderful Jesus." To accompany him as he sang it, as only he could, and then to play it for a congregation of two thousand was something I have never quite forgotten. I recall that he altered the last line of the chorus the last time through from "in the heart" to "in *thy* heart."

Mr. Wm. E. Branton, A.R.C.O.

■   I could tell many stories about him. My best is that once he was preaching in Northgate Street, Gloucester, and the place was packed to capacity. Suddenly dear old Gipsy stood up and said "Gentlemen, be gentlemen, please." Every man who could possibly stand

up did so, for women to sit down. It was a wonderful
sight to see. Almost unbelievable!

Rev. Ronald Taylor

■ I attended his meetings in Glasgow in March,
1923, and am happy to tell you what I know of him
and his influence on my life. I had been brought up
in a good home with parents inclined to religious things,
but perhaps lacking knowledge of personal salvation.
Serving in the 1914-18 war, latterly as an officer, I had
a rather wild life. In 1923, a Christian man I knew in
the army suggested that I should go and hear Gipsy
Smith on a Sunday at St. Andrew's Hall, Glasgow,
which I did. The Gipsy's very informal approach and
obvious reality arrested me; and when he sang "Wonderful Jesus," I was immediately impressed by the
realization that this man knew Jesus Christ as a real
living person. I went straight home after that and in my
room asked God to make Jesus real to me like that.
From that time, I began reading my Bible and learning the way of salvation more perfectly. Only once after that did I hear the Gipsy—when he was in Glasgow,
some years later. I think he was greatly used by God;
and although he was accused of being too emotional, I
believe his very sincerity and directness were needed at
that time, as I think they are needed now.

Two remarks made by him I think are typical. He
was asked in America if he would accept a D.D. and
when told what the initials meant, he declined and said
that his divinity didn't need a doctor. On another occasion, he asked a minister how many members he had
in his church; and when the minister replied, "Nomi-

nally 600," the Gipsy had to look up the dictionary for
the meaning of *nominal* and found it given as unreal.

He was a very attractive personality, and I am sure
has gone to a very real commendation from the Master
whom he loved and served.

Mr. William Macfarlane

■ I was one of the young people who responded to
the urging of the late Mr. W. E. Gundry, of Sydney
Technical College, to hear Gipsy Smith, during his
visit to Australia in the mid-nineteen twenties.

The Sydney Hippodrome was packed with people of
all ages for the evening meetings. The tall evangelist
was a commanding figure as he stood on an elevated
platform. Near him were forty people who had been
converted at his mission on a previous visit thirty years
earlier. There was a heart-warming appeal in the very
presence of the big man with a genial expression on his
face, as he announced the hymns from the songbook
Wonderful Jesus and Other Songs, my copy of which is
by my side now in my study as I type these memories.
When Gipsy Smith read the opening lines of the hymns
and called on the people to sing, with a sweeping
movement of his raised right arm, there was a resound-
ing response all around that large boxing stadium. He
created an uplifting atmosphere of praise and prayer.

I had made a public decision for Christ at a Sunday
school mission campaign conducted by Mr. Cumming,
the Scottish evangelist, in Sydney several years previous-
ly. This was followed later by a deep spiritual experience of the meaning of love to God. Something more
was needed. Gipsy Smith's meetings provided the inspiration. It was as if I were walking on air as I left the

meeting one night with the words ringing in my ears, "Believe on the Lord Jesus Christ and thou shalt be saved."

Since my ordination to the Christian ministry in 1934, I have mentioned Gipsy Smith many times in sermons, including his illustration about the boy who attempted to accept the minister's handshake at the church door, with his right fist full of marbles, pointing to the necessity of coming to God with an open hand.

Rev. Geoffrey Hope Hume

GIPSY SMITH ON TOUR. Starting off for his thirty-third evangelistic campaign in the USA in August 1936

30

Bells Across Elizabeth

God knows where to deposit investment for eternity.

Ten thousand people flocked into Epping Forest one day in June 1935, when the Gipsy conducted an open air meeting near the spot where he was born. Appropriately enough, the Gipsy used a gypsy wagon as his pulpit. His dear wife, Annie, sat inside the wagon, and many memories must have crowded her mind, too. He talked about his life and, with the leafy trees as a canopy, the meeting gave one a sense of what it must have been like when great crowds came to hear Jesus. The gathering at Epping certainly could have made a fine finish to the evangelist's labors. But, soon afterward, he was crossing the Atlantic once more. "I'll preach my Saviour while I've breath," was very much the Gipsy's personal creed.

One of the great events of the 1936 American tour was the campaign at Elizabeth, New Jersey. It was here that a chorus "Sixty Years of Service" was written as a tribute to the Gipsy. The "revival campaign" (as the newspapers called it) was organized by the Elizabeth Council of Churches, Ministers' Association and YMCA, and held in a large auditorium, the Armory of the 114th Infantry. The choir alone numbered nearly four hundred, and large crowds came to hear the revivalist. The Gipsy had trouble with the microphone here, too—but God had given him a strong voice which needed little, if any, amplification.

For five minutes every night of the campaign, all the churches in Elizabeth rang their bells to announce the meetings. On the first night, Gipsy Smith explained why he had come to Elizabeth. The *Elizabeth Daily Journal* reported that "he said that he wants revived churches, stronger Christian sentiment and attitude in the homes . . . honesty and straightforward dealing with God and with man. He emphasized the point that church membership alone is not sufficient, saying that the primary need is for persons to be converted." He certainly emphasized the need for godly living.

"Every time you drink, you help the devil," he told an audience of two thousand. And he told a women's rally that America's greatest need was godly mothers, not women who were "painted dolls" or "clothes horses."

Yet, he was no killjoy. As the local newspaper reported of the meeting in which the evangelist recounted his war experiences; "Gipsy Smith flayed the prudishness of the church and condemned the clergymen who believe that one cannot be a follower of God unless he has a Bible in one hand and a 'Hail Jehovah' on his lips. He said that one of the biggest things that most people could do for the church was to leave the church service smiling."

The Elizabeth campaign *did* prove to be a revival. At the close of the fortnight's meetings, five thousand people crowded the Armory to hear the Gipsy's final address, a sermon on Acts chapter 16, from the twenty-fifth verse. His parting words were an expression of his entire life: "don't be satisfied with a little Christianity—get *all* you can."

Hundreds of decision cards were signed during the campaign, and churches all over the town had been revived and encouraged. Fifteen thousand copies of the *Gipsy Smith Hymn Book* were sold or given away during the fortnight, and not a single copy of the evangelist's autobiography remained on the bookstall. But more significant to the life of the churches in Elizabeth were the words of Dr. S. N. Reeves, Ph.D., at the very beginning of the campaign:

"The coming of Gipsy Smith to Elizabeth is a distinct and clear challenge to the spirit of Christian unity in our midst. The call of Christ is heard now with commanding impressiveness, 'All ye are brethren.' Are we? The opportunity is ours to demonstrate that we are, by the united way in which we give God's messenger the right of way in our lives during these fifteen days."

Such unity came, and remained after the Gipsy had moved on. In our day, when Christian unity is so dominant an issue, Dr. Reeves' words have a prophetic ring about them. "All ye are brethren"—and the spirit of unity springs from that earnest, compelling desire to bring others to Christ.

There was a warm, pleasant touch about the Elizabeth campaign. On the sixtieth anniversary of his conversion, the organizing committee presented the evangelist with a basket of sixty roses. The choir, not to be left out, presented him with an umbrella "to combat the rains of England."

The Elizabeth campaign was one of many. It would be a life's work for any biographer to try to trace all that the Gipsy did in America, let alone the rest of the world. But it presents us with an interesting picture of an evangelist, still going strong at seventy-six years of age. On that anniversary night, the choir sang the Gipsy's favorite song, "He is Mine."

The Elizabeth campaign was one of many conducted during this thirty-third American tour. Other meetings were held in Dallas, where Gipsy spoke at the Centenary Fair (a visit that resulted in the signing of some 10,000 decision cards) as well as in Buffalo and Honolulu. He was also made an honorary Indian chief and proudly brought back to England a feathered headdress in which he looked very handsome.

Why did the Gipsy love the USA so much? Cynics suggested that the money was the main attraction. The real reason is certainly the enthusiasm for evangelism that he found in the USA, for, as he told his English friends, "the energy they [the Americans] put into revival meetings knows no bounds." They expected much, and gained much, as may be observed from a cablegram received by the Gipsy on board the *S.S. Majestic* as he returned from the USA. The leaders of the churches in Winston-Salem, North Carolina, had together composed the cablegram: "the spirit of our churches has been transformed. The dominant note is that the beauty of Jesus may be seen in them."

Gipsy certainly did more radio work in the USA than he did in England, though his first radio broadcast was in his home country—in the very early days of radio. On that occasion, he did not feel at ease, talking into a strange object that looked like a tin box, and with no congregation before him. However, he was encouraged to use the emerging medium, and became a very effective broadcaster. Many radio stations across the USA invited the Gipsy to the microphone, but one of the high spots in his radio career was the broadcast from Brooklyn, New York, in the early nineteen-thirties, when he was the guest of the Reverend Dr. Parkes Cadman. The British radio system, organized as a state-sponsored corporation, offered somewhat less opportunity to the evangelist, but—as you will see in the next chapter—another member of the family conquered the kingdom of the air-waves in a quite unexpected way.

GIPSY SMITH PREACHING. Addressing a group from a gypsy caravan in Epping Forest, Essex, England

31

A Very Special Romany

*What a wonderful thing a tree is! A poem in trunk,
branches, twigs and leaves. A bouquet in spring and
a basket of fruit in autumn. Listen to its heart and it
will tell you of a cradle and a coffin—a city of birds
and a shelter for man and beast.*

Gipsy Smith had a very special affection for his
nephew Bram, to whom the world-famous evangelist
was Uncle Rodney. Bram or, to give his full name,
the Reverend George Bramwell Evens, was ordained
a Wesleyan Methodist minister at Cardiff in 1908. He
was Tilly's son, and inherited many qualities from his
grandfather, Cornelius. Like the Gipsy, George Bramwell Evens had what some call the power of natural
oratory. His interest in the world of nature excelled
that even of his Uncle Rodney, however. Bram must
have thought over a few sermons as he sat by the river-
side, waiting for a bite, or lingered under a tree, hoping
to catch sight of one of the wild animals he so superb-
ly described in his BBC radio broadcasts. Certainly, he
acquired a vast knowledge of the ways of the wild and
developed, albeit unconsciously, the knack of holding
an audience's attention while describing the deeds of a
young badger, or an otter, or some other creature.

It seemed natural enough, that this tall, dark-eyed

233

minister, possessor of a *vardo* (a real Romany gypsy wagon) should share his love of nature with others. Requests for talks came from schools and children's groups but, just like Uncle Rodney, Bram was as much at home with an individual as with a crowd. Like the Gipsy, too, he had a talent for expressing his thoughts in print. Over the years, the evangelist wrote many articles and books, but Bram concentrated on the world of nature for that, after all, is another way of seeing God in all His wondrous ways! He first appeared in print with articles for provincial papers and for *The Methodist Recorder*. Some of these later appeared as collections, in book form.

To say that he was rather unorthodox by prevailing standards could be an understatement, though a gently-meant one. He delighted in wearing old and beloved clothes in the pursuit of some new knowledge about wild animals. A keen photographer and bird watcher, he brought to the pulpit his spontaneous gratitude for all the beauty that God has put into this world. It would have been impossible for him to imagine a heaven without his animal friends. He was a very happy man; a Christian who delighted in God's creation. It was hardly surprising that he tended to be absentminded about trivial matters such as his hat, which he was forever leaving behind him at meetings.

He was nearly fifty years of age when, as the result of one of those encounters which we call chance, he was invited to broadcast on the BBC radio program, "Children's Hour." The year was 1933 and broadcasting was in its infancy. Everyone at the BBC program was called by their Christian name with the prefix "Aunt" or "Uncle." But "Uncle Bramwell" didn't seem to fit. So, at his own suggestion, they called him "Romany." It became one of the most famous names in radio. As he was a keen member of the Gypsy Lore Society*, the the name was appropriate enough.

The program format developed into a simple ramble, "Out with Romany," when the broadcaster and his friends, to say nothing of his beloved spaniel, Raq, went for a walk in the country. It was a studio production, of course, but, with the skillful use of sound effects and the "come and see this" approach of Romany, listeners believed that it was an outside broadcast. In their mind's eye, millions of adults and children who listened really went out with Romany. When it was suggested the afternoon program be moved to the evening for a wider adult audience, the obvious response came. It would be dark at night—how would Romany see all the creatures he described on the program? After many years of broadcasts, a publicity feature reported that it *was* a studio production, but many regular listeners probably didn't believe *that*. Romany would have been happy to take the microphone into the woods, but outside broadcasts were not so easily produced then, as now, and the pressure was always on to plan the next program.

In addition, Romany, still a hard-working minister, was in great demand around the churches, where he gave countless talks (always called "Out with Romany"). He would talk about his animal and human friends, drawing quick sketches on the blackboard to illustrate his point. Then, at the end of his talk, he

* A beautifully written and illustrated book on gypsies in Britain was written by Dora E. Yates, for many years honorary secretary to the Gypsy Lore Society. The book, *My Gypsy Days,* was published by Phoenix House of London in 1953.

would ask the children if they would like to see Raq, who would have been left in the vestry, or in an adjoining room, in a comfortable basket. The famous dog always knew when it was time to bound up the steps into the pulpit, and into his master's arms, by the roar of children's voices. Yes, they *always* wanted to see Raq.

Romany was not a great evangelist like his uncle. His special ministry was a cheerful appraisal of this world. It is entirely scriptural to point to nature as demonstration of God's great bounty; Jesus did so frequently. When one had heard Romany, the nature hymns, like "All Things Bright and Beautiful," had an extra significance. He was besieged by children. Letters came daily asking Romany's advice about the choice of a pet (a dog like Raq, for example) or seeking knowledge about some wild animal. Sometimes, there were more personal pleas for help from people in some distress or anguish.

The heavy mailbag was dealt with by Romany's wife, who wrote a very fine biography of her husband (*Through the Years with Romany,* by Eunice Evens: University of London Press, 1946) after his death. He worked on "Children's Hour" for ten years and, to the end of his life, remained natural and responsive to children. It probably never occurred to him that he was famous.

The letters received by Romany were not all requests for help or advice. Many related personal experiences, nature lore or legend—thoughts that Romany might weave into his popular radio program. One memory recently reported to the author shows the kind of letter that pleased Romany most. It came from an avid listener to his program:

■ "Once, they (Romany and his dog, Raq, plus his friends, Muriel and Doris) were gathering blackberries and eating them, i.e. during the broadcast. I wrote to Romany saying how very surprised I was that he would eat blackberries in October. Did he not know that the devil put his cloven hoof on them in September? Also Romany and his friends ate berries that had a spider's web over them, covered for fairies. This is true, not legend—I was gathering this fruit one day and I came across a jar of blackberry jam labeled 'for the fairies.' Romany answered my letter and thanked me for the lovely legends. Yes, I looked forward to his 'Children's Hour' programs."

Mrs. M. M. Entwistle

Romany was a faithful minister of the gospel, in addition to being a highly successful communicator. In our ecology-conscious world, his message would have had an added relevance.

Gipsy Smith, born nearly a quarter of a century before Romany, thought that his nephew might "inherit the mantle." As it was, Romany died first, quickly and quietly, after working in his garden. When the news was broadcast on November 20, 1943, millions of people experienced a real sense of loss. It was hard to realize that there would be no more walks with Romany. He was fifty-nine when he finished his life's work, a natural broadcaster who radiated a natural delight with what lies all about us.

Someone who heard Romany at Hull, where the Gipsy did so much work, those years before, expressed the truth simply enough: "It was a great trail."

32

The Beloved Biographer

When God has big business on hand, faith always gets the contract.

To be truthful, Harold Murray was more a chronicler than a biographer. Countless articles appeared in the English church papers, notably the *Methodist Recorder,* under the brief byline "H.M." Almost everyone knew who H.M. was. A freelance journalist and pianist, he became actively involved in the Gipsy's work soon after the First World War. At the time he was very much on his own with virtually no plans for the future. The Gipsy gave him the simple invitation, "Why not come around with me?" And so it was that H.M. enjoyed the Gipsy's friendship for some thirty years.

Few people could have known the Gipsy so well, warts and all. The invitation did not spring from any desire for extra publicity on the Gipsy's part. If anything, he suffered from too much publicity. But he knew the importance of having an accompanist who understood the evangelist's needs. During the American tours, Edwin Young acted as pianist, and wrote some fine choruses as well. But the Gipsy had discovered that some organists and pianists in British churches felt they could not "descend" to playing choruses or "hymn tunes that sounded like a jig." If the evangelist had any fixed ideas about church music, it was that joy should be the keynote. He had no time for fussy choirs who tried to tell the Gipsy what to do!

"Some choirs rehearse so much that they rehearse out all the spontaneous joy of praising the Lord," he said. "The results are word perfect but spiritually stifling!"

The Gipsy had a favorite note on the keyboard. When asked the secret of his success, he would go to the piano and strike B natural (be natural). He had much in common with Dr. F. Luke Wiseman, who also accompanied the Gipsy at the piano from time to time. Harold Murray said that they shared a love for melodious congregational singing. Not unexpectedly, the Gipsy encountered a few out-of-tune pianos during his campaigns around Britain. "I think every chord in that one is a lost chord!" he would say. And the stewards would immediately promise to get the instrument tuned before the next meeting.

"That must be a very valuable piano," he would smile, "and I'm sure that a museum would be very pleased to have it!" The Gipsy was not standing on his dignity, of course. He recognized the importance of the ministry of song, and likewise thought that an out-of-tune piano meant an out-of-tune church. For all his spontaneity, the Gipsy was a man who liked to see all things done in order. He hated threadbare worship.

"This is the Lord's house," he would tell his congregation. "Shouldn't we furnish it as well as our own?"

Harold Murray was able to ease the way, as far as many of these matters were concerned. Sometimes, churches did not realize that the Gipsy would want to use the piano, which they kept just as a standby or as something to stand flowers on.

Although he often sang to organ accompaniment, the Gipsy preferred the piano. The words, he thought, were easier to hear. Songs were sung in unlikely places. Harold Murray reported one occasion on which the Gipsy and Dr. Wiseman sang a duet at Liskeard railway station at midnight—without piano accompaniment, of course.

Harold Murray traveled all over Britain, playing for the Gipsy and sending dispatches to the church newspapers. They were adventurous years, although the reporter was sometimes prompted to defend the Gipsy's approach to money, for example. Like so many evangelists, he faced criticism over the matter of payment. Then, as now, churches too often expected their preachers "on the cheap."

"Count Your Blessings" was often used as the collection hymn. The Gipsy would point out that counting your blessings was different from counting your small change and putting the smallest in the plate.

Once he told a congregation that they should not sing the words "Love so amazing, so divine, demands my soul, my life, my all" unless every person put at least a half-crown in the collection. It was not that the evangelist was avaricious. He had the gypsies' shrewdness and people too often forgot that he really *was* a gypsy. He needed an adequate income to pay for all his work, but never asked for a penny for himself or his family. As Harold Murray pointed out, he often gave his time without payment, and spent little money on himself. Sometimes, a church might take £100 in collections during a visit by the Gipsy, but he would take only his expenses. In America, the evangelist put a strict limit on what he would accept.

However, he did hammer home this matter of giving. "Are you going to give less to the church than you give to the cinema or the cigarette manufacturer?" he would ask. It was because the question was so relevant that people disliked it. Blaming the Gipsy for thinking only about money was, too often, a way of explaining away one's own stinginess in this matter.

"You hang onto that sixpence so much you give it a headache," he might say, referring to the King's inscription. Or, "When the collection is announced, too many of us act like the hymn title, 'There'll Be No Parting There.'"

Some would say that this concern with giving had an adverse effect on the Gipsy's reputation. Any critic had best look at his own work for God first, however, and then recall the Gipsy's life ministry. No sum of money can make up for months and years away from one's home and family, in the cause of the gospel.

Harold Murray found a very telling quotation among the writings of Mark Twain, the American novelist. Referring to a missionary meeting, Mark Twain said, "When the speaker had talked for ten minutes, I was so impressed that I decided to give every cent I had with me. Ten minutes later, I decided I wouldn't give anything and, at the end of the talk when the plate came round, I was so exhausted by the argument that I extracted two dollars for my own use." Well, the Gipsy certainly did not leave people feeling like that!

Harold Murray really deserves a book to himself, since he so ably shared the Gipsy's work through the medium of print. It was Harold Murray who wrote up the Gipsy's American campaigns for British audiences and, like the Gipsy, had a simple, direct approach.

"People don't want to read dull, heavy, theological arguments," he wrote. "They want to read of bold, aggressive efforts to bring about evangelical revival, effort in which there is sacrifice and reality."

A gifted artist (who once decorated a storefront window with scenes from the gospels), Harold Murray wrote a number of books about eminent preachers, including G. Campbell Morgan and Dinsdale T. Young. In addition, he published—privately—many books and booklets about Christian work and evangelism. He gave so many of these away that it is doubtful that he ever made a profit. On the other hand, he had the satisfaction of knowing that he was helping keep alive the promise of God's blessing upon sacrificial, hope-filled evangelism.

In 1937, Harold Murray put together some of his experiences in *Sixty Years an Evangelist: an Intimate Study of Gipsy Smith*. A handsome paperback, costing just a shilling, it had to be reprinted within a couple of months of publication. It was a best-seller of its kind and a remarkably fresh picture of the seventy-six-year-old crusader. Full of anecdotes and memories of campaigns, the book reminds one that a comprehensive biographer of Gipsy Smith would need a lifetime to tackle the job (and even then, he probably wouldn't manage to tell *all* the story).

A special meeting was held at Westminster in London as part of these sixtieth anniversary celebrations, and Lloyd George, a friend of the Gipsy for many years, came along to say a few words. Mr. J. Ogden, a jeweler, on behalf of a few of the Gipsy's closest friends, presented him with a beautiful silver model of a gypsy wagon. This had been designed by his grandson, Rodney James Lean, as a biscuit barrel. It took the evangelist by surprise—he just gazed at it in wonder. If there was any outstandingly endearing quality of this man, it was the open expression of his true emotions. Just watching him, that day, everyone could tell how much the gift meant to him.

In writing his book, Harold Murray paid tribute to the Gipsy's wife, Annie, then in her seventy-ninth year. But before the book was published, she died. Dear Annie, always behind the scenes, but always one in spirit with her husband. Unassuming, gentle, always ready to welcome the visitor, expected or unexpected, Annie was called to face all the special problems of being an evangelist's wife. Sometimes, she hardly knew where her husband would be on any particular day, such was the pace of his work. But always she was confident that the good Lord would bring him home safely. Her children had crowned her life with satisfaction, too: Hanley had become a Methodist minister (Gipsy and his son often used to share the same pulpit), while Albany became a gypsy evangelist in his own right in America.

Zillah married a bank manager, Mr. James Lean of Redruth, in Cornwall, although they subsequently moved to Cambridge to be near her mother. Annie traveled widely with the Gipsy in the early years of their marriage, but that proved difficult in her later life. She loved England. The wonderful scenery of other lands impressed her, but, as she said in her modest way, "England is good enough." When Annie died, it was the end of an era. Somehow, the Gipsy felt that he had to move on and, on the advice of his son, Albany, he sold Romany Tan, the home which he and Annie had for so long shared.

Harold Murray recalled that the Gipsy was in America, in the midst of a campaign, when his wife died. Probably, he added, it would have been her wish that her death should not interfere with the Gipsy's important task. It would have been so much like her.

During most of those sixty years, Gipsy Smith had been able to count on the support and care of his wife. Though she stayed in the background, Annie may well have been his greatest strength on earth, although she herself was not robust. In the early days of his ministry, he read his sermons to her, to see if they were good enough!

"That, and better, will do," she had told him. Perhaps she knew, after all, the life to which the Lord called her.

Harold Murray outlived the Gipsy. Disabled by a cerebral hemmorrage but well cared for in a home for old people, he died in 1960, and, almost to the end, talked about the great days of campaigns with Gipsy Smith, Samuel Chadwick, and the rest.

Mary Alice

*No man can look long into the face of Jesus without,
when he looks at his brother, loving Him.*

It came like a bombshell! The Gipsy was marrying
again and a woman fifty years younger than himself!
Remarkable as it must seem now, very many people
forgot the many years of service performed by this
valiant warrior for God, and took an uncharitable view
of this unexpected second marriage. Pagans, in a con-
temporary Antioch, might well say "behold how these
Christians judge one another."

Mary Alice Shaw was a university graduate in English literature—and a warm-hearted Christian. It was
on her twenty-seventh birthday that she married the
evangelist in California on July 2, 1938. Inevitably, it
was front-page news; and once more the Gipsy had to
bear the burden of publicity, though much newspaper
comment was kindly.

Anyone who knew the Gipsy well recognized the age-
less warmth of spirit that he possessed. In his seventies
and eighties, he certainly knew a weariness of body
but never of mind. But he surprised them! He surprised
those earnest, respectable churchgoers who thought
that the Gipsy should conform to their pattern. He did
not, because he could not. His way of life necessitated

a helpmeet. If he had taken a housekeeper, some people would have found reason to criticize. In fact, the second marriage extended the Gipsy's ministry. Dr. Oswald Smith of Toronto wrote of Mary, that she was a great comfort to the Gipsy during the later years of his life. "Every moment of her time was devoted to his happiness."

Harold Murray certainly had a high opinion of Mary and considered her "a capable, highly-educated, practical Christian." One day, he asked Mary what she did in the meetings.

"Pray for him," she replied. She was very much a helpmeet, however, handling his secretarial work, sometimes acting as soloist and even taking meetings—all this in addition to caring for the Gipsy, remember! At the end of his eventful life, Mary said of him, "He belongs to the world." As indeed, he did.

Just as the evangelist worked for the cause of Anglo-American relations during the First World War, when he traveled some 50,000 miles through the USA, so did he respond to that important task in the Second. He and Mary went all over North America, conducting meetings and telling that world-famous testimony of the gospel in the gypsy tent! For England remained in his thoughts and prayers, but it was impossible for him to return home while the war continued.

Gipsy's engagement book was certainly crowded during the early 1940s, but after 1942 the time between campaigns lengthened. He no longer possessed the physical vigor evident ten years earlier. Yet, among his many 1942 engagements are listed missions at Birmingham, Minnesota; Calvary Baptist Church, New York; Minneapolis; Los Angeles; and of course, Chi-

cago, a city for which he had much affection. His letters home to England speak of crowded buildings, enthusiastic congregations and churches, with scores and
even hundreds going into the inquiry room. He was, as
usual, greatly heartened and impressed by the cooperation of ministers and city officials. Perhaps, in those
early wartime years, the Gipsy's message came into its
own once more: in a world of hatred and ugliness,
God's love remained the supreme, unalterable reality.

But his pace was slackening—which is hardly surprising when one considers the age of this remarkable
man. In 1944, the year in which he campaigned at
Augusta and Atlanta, Georgia; Los Angeles; New York;
Ocean Grove; and elsewhere, he wrote, somewhat re-
flectively, from Marion, Ohio, to his family in England.
A portion of the letter (kindly reproduced by permis-
sion of his granddaughter) has something of the Gipsy's
poetic flourish to the impending close of a great career:

> We had a wonderful time in Marion. . . . The
> meetings were really wonderful, from first to last,
> outstanding. [There were] fifty-six ministers with
> their churches behind them, and literally hundreds
> gave themselves to the Lord at each meeting. Just
> to show you the impression made upon the whole
> country: there is a big training camp close to the
> city with thousands of men getting ready for over-
> seas. They had advertised a blackout and mock air
> raid over the city in the afternoon of the last Sunday.
> When the military authorities realized that a meet-
> ing of five thousand would be gathered in the City
> Hall to hear the gospel, they placed a notice in the
> Saturday and Sunday papers [to state] that the air
> raid alert was postponed until further notice so that

the people could be with us and not be disturbed by an excitement which might not help my message and the spirit of the revival. This gave a great boost to the last day of the mission. We thanked God and took courage.

The Gipsy continued, having reflected on the recent death of his old friend, Dr. Luke Wiseman (Home Missions Secretary of the Methodist Church in Britain),

I begin to feel somehow the shadows of the night seem to be coming nearer. I have lived through the springtime, rainbow hues of summer, the beauty and glory, the satisfying golden harvests, the rigors of winter. I now face a new spring, the dawn which shall be eternal. I shall see them all [i.e. his friends who had already gone to be with the Lord] again, and I shall see Him whom I have served and loved and tried to lift up and preach, the sinner's friend and Saviour and Lord, see Him face to face and tell the story, saved by grace.

Following the campaign at Marion, the Gipsy was to have gone on to Philadelphia and Massachusetts, but campaigns at both places were canceled to give the Gipsy essential rest. Eyewitness accounts of the Gipsy's missions in his final years clearly indicate that he was but a shadow of his former self. But that he remained a spiritual giant and retained his humor cannot be in doubt. In the end, all diligent workers for the Lord lose much of their "get up and go" because of this human frame. Maybe it is because they are finally called to "get up and go" to the Lord.

This new sense of his departing throws a new light on his return to England in 1945. Some might have thought the trip foolhardy for a man in his mid-eighties, but it is more likely that he wanted a final look at those scenes associated with his great missions of former decades. In his visit to his birthplace, for instance, it was a matter of reflecting anew "what God hath wrought." Had the Gipsy been spared to preach in the USA after that memorable visit to England, it could have been only as a postscript to a remarkable story.

Indeed, when the Gipsy *did* return to England in 1945, it represented another great surprise. Many people had believed him dead. His ministry in those war years was a result of his wife's care and constant attention. The doctors said that he ought to retire but, as we have seen, the Gipsy acted on the words of that old hymn, "I'll Praise My Saviour While I've Breath." And so he did. He preached in London and also went back to Hanley, full of memories still, though so many old friends had gone on to glory, as the Gipsy put it. His message remained that of joyful Christian living—and why we should settle for nothing less!

A man so near the gates of heaven must have felt keenly the need for revived churches and consecrated individuals. But England in those postwar years was weary, preoccupied with ration books, making ends meet, trying to recover from a devastating war. The Gipsy went to see the hornbeam tree in Epping Forest, the landmark of his birthplace which, fortunately, had survived bombing in the area.

In those last two years of the evangelist's life, Mary did all that she could to make him comfortable. God, in his wisdom, had given the Gipsy a young wife; an older woman could never have stood up to the strain of day and night nursing. They lived in a small flat in

London, and the Gipsy felt imprisoned, as that young lad, Rodney, who had come to London to work for William Booth so long ago.

Some of his friends looked for a place in the country, but accommodation, like so much else, was almost impossible to find. At eighty-seven, the evangelist remained lively, in possession of his faculties, but his voice and his heart were failing. It was a hard decision to take, but his friends thought he would stand a better chance of recovery in America—a season in the Florida sunshine. Of course, he *was* the same indomitable man. His last tour in America had included fifty or sixty campaigns.

"I've had a good inning," he told visitors who came to see him during his period in a London hospital. The Gipsy told one of his visitors that he "fancied a plate of tripe." He could still smile.

So it was in the summer of 1947, that Mary Alice and Gipsy Smith boarded the *Queen Mary,* on its first postwar trip to New York.

How different it was from all those other departures! Quiet prayer rather than rousing cheers for the Gipsy followed the ship out of Southampton. Yet, there was an air of celebration, since the *Queen Mary's* departure seemed to symbolize better days to come. The flags were flying. They were flying, too, in New York, as Britain's most famous liner concluded its voyage, on August 4. But the Gipsy had gone on to another welcome. Mary's very special ministry was over.

Epilogue

Newspapers were slim in Britain then. News had to be *big* news to make even page two or three of a four-page edition. In addition, the Gipsy had been away from England during the war years; he rated a low priority in Fleet Street, the heart of Britain's newspaper empire. His death was announced on the radio and, like all other events, became yesterday's news.

All over England and, indeed all over the world, people wept to hear the news but rejoiced that the Gipsy had been spared for such a long and fruitful ministry. He had known great preachers of this century and the last, and worked with them. He had brought countless thousands to Christ. He had preached in downtown America, in the diamond fields of South Africa, in youthful, exuberant Australia, in English suburbia and in more places than any man could count. He had loved greatly and been greatly loved. He had been misunderstood, but had himself understood the reason for such misunderstanding. He rejoiced in the open book of nature and in the open book of the Bible. He had been born in a gypsy tent to preach to millions, and his ashes, at his request, were buried under the hornbeam tree in the forest from whence he came. There will never be anyone quite like Gipsy Smith.

On July 2, 1949, a memorial was unveiled at Mill Plain, Epping Forest. This four feet high piece of

Cornish granite bears the emblem of a gypsy wagon
and the inscription:

> *Gipsy Rodney Smith, M.B.E., who preached the*
> *Gospel to thousands on five continents for 70 years,*
> *was born here March 31st 1860, and called home,*
> *journeying to America, August 4th 1947.*

WHAT HATH GOD WROUGHT

He was the world's most popular preacher for more
than seventy years. Some might argue that such a
man would not appeal to our sophisticated age. They
overlook the climate in which Gipsy Smith often labored. Examine the environment of his work in his
time and you will find the same old problems of reaching the outsider and reconciling Christians.

"If you want revival," he said, "draw a chalk circle
around yourself and pray, 'God, begin revival inside
this ring.'"

He would not want our praise now. He would only
want us to take his message seriously.

Harold Murray wrote a small memoir in aid of Cliff
College funds, some short time after the evangelist's
death. A line in the book would have made a fitting
epitaph: "This one thing he did—he made religion attractive!" Most of us are still struggling to understand
the secret of *that* ministry.

Evaluation: His Ministry and Ours

"Don't try to put the Gipsy in a stained glass window." This advice was passed along to the writer by a publisher. Well, if there is any sign of stained glass window in this little book, the Gipsy would certainly ask for it to be removed in order to let in a little fresh air. Even now, some people make much of the evangelist's so-called failings—his emotionalism, his concern with the collection and the way in which he married again. Christ is always more ready to forgive than many of us, who say that we are His followers.

Looking at the Gipsy's ministry is a useful exercise, since we are so deeply involved in our own communication problem. The Gipsy would have laughed had we told him that we fail to reach the people.

"They're behind those front doors," he'd say. "Try knocking on them." And, as we can see, he never waited for people to come into the church on his terms. Had he done so, he might well have preached to a couple dozen people at the Batty Circus to the end of his days. He had a special regard for open-air work— and for the unconventional. "Surprise them!" That was his approach to preaching and it was his approach to the ministry. In that he was very much in accord with the sense of the gospels, in which we read that people were astonished, amazed, surprised, at all that Jesus said and did.

He never forgot the spiritual climate within the churches. Prayer meetings, to him, were not an optional extra, to be dropped in favor of bazaars or choir practice. Prayer created the spiritual climate of obedience and expectancy, in which the Holy Spirit would work. And where that was lacking, the Gipsy rightly admonished those who were too often absent servants of the Lord. He loved preaching, and he loved the church. There was no dragging of the feet up the pulpit steps, and he immediately awakened the spiritually snoozing congregations of his day. He'd say something like, "Have you come here to get a blessing? Good. So have I."

He did not diminish the authority of the pulpit. But he bridged that terrifying gap between the pulpit and the pew—and that was the reason why people listened to him.

No one could call the Gipsy an intellectual. Unlike some intellectuals, the Gipsy preached a positive faith. His theology was simple but sound. The only question mark left in the hearer's mind was what he, personally, was going to do about it.

He was emotional, of course. The well-worn criticism of preachers could be applied to Gipsy Smith readily enough. But it was a real emotion! Whatever else could be said of him, he was very much what he appeared to be. Facing this question of emotionalism, he reminded his audience that, while it was quite acceptable to cheer footballers or politicians, it was somehow held to be out of place to cheer in church. He could never see the logic in an artificially restrained religion, in the pulpit or in the pew.

The arguments about his views on the giving of Christians will continue, because few of us are the kind of stewards we ought to be. This was at the heart of the evangelist's message. He did not grow wealthy from religion in the sense that his critics meant. For example, he had to maintain a home, even during those months and years that he never saw it. An evangelist with his kind of ministry always has a heavy expense account.

It is certain that he refused very many offers of well-paid pastorates in America, because he believed that his task of evangelism overruled all else.

Like all great evangelists, he was in many ways misunderstood and thereby lonely. His second marriage demonstrates that, clearer than any other aspect of his life. It is the philosophy of the world rather than of the way of Christ that we have to judge those who do not act as we would. But it is easier to think of Gipsy Smith in heaven than it is of those who judged him so harshly. None of us merit a place there; we claim Jesus Christ's worthiness, not our own, whoever we are and whatever our ministry. The final criterion is what a man leaves behind him. More than twenty years after the Gipsy's death, many people continue to thank God that they heard the evangelist. Many preachers this Sunday will stand in pulpits and build up the church, as the result of coming to Christ during the Gipsy's ministry.

Shortly before his death, Gipsy Smith broadcast on BBC radio, recalling the prayer of a farmer at one of his very first campaigns, nearly seventy years before. The farmer, prophesying that the youthful evangelist would travel all over the world and be greatly used for God's work, prayed, "Keep him low, Lord, keep him low."

"And, do you know?" the Gipsy said in that final broadcast. "We have to be kept low if the Lord is to use us."

For myself, concerned with the problems of using mass media to reach *our* unconcerned neighbors, I find in Gipsy Smith, as in Romany Evens, a new understanding of what it means to reach out and touch that someone across the street, or in the rear pew, or idly listening to a car radio.

It will never be possible to report all that the Gipsy did and said. Let the Gipsy's final word to us here be his most potent challenge to the church in our generation: "Can others see Jesus in you?"

Moody Press, a ministry of the Moody Bible Institute, is designed for education, evangelization and edification. If we may assist you in knowing more about Christ and the Christian life, please write us without obligation to: Moody Press, c/o MLM, Chicago, Illinois 60610.